Tom Hunt

THE NATURAL COOK:

Eating the
seasons from
root to fruit

Photography by
Laura Edwards

QUADRILLE

For my grans, Dodo and Anita, who first taught me how to cook.

Editorial director Anne Furniss

Creative director Helen Lewis

Editors Simon Davis and Lucy Bannell

Designer Nicola Ellis

Design assistants Emily Lapworth and Gemma Hogan

Photographer Laura Edwards

Stylist Tabitha Hawkins

Illustrator Katie Horwich

Production controller Leonie Kellman

Production director Vincent Smith

First published in 2014 by
Quadrille Publishing Limited
Pentagon House
52 to 54 Southwark Street
London SE1 1UN
www.quadrille.co.uk
www.quadrile.com

Reprinted in 2016
10 9 8 7 6 5 4 3 2

Quadrille is an imprint of Hardie Grant
www.hardiegrant.com.au

Text © 2014 Tom Hunt

Photography © 2014 Laura Edwards

Design and layout © 2014 Quadrille
Publishing Limited

ISBN 978 1 84949 733 6

Printed in China

CONTENTS

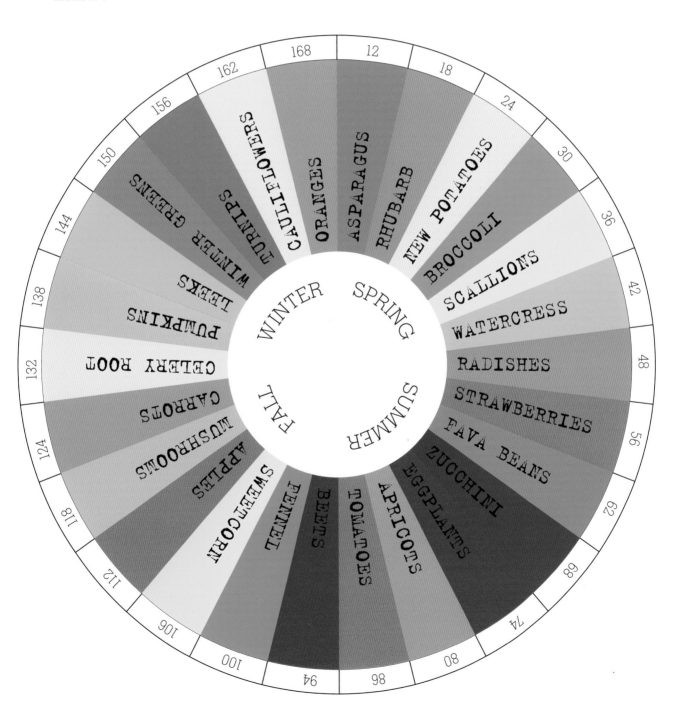

How I cook

I love cooking simple, rustic food that is full of flavor, vibrant, and healthy. All good meals start with the ingredients so, before I start cooking, I seek out the very best I can. You'll find me hunting the market for the crispest, boldest, most stunning vegetables, the best-marbled cheaper cuts of meat, and glassy-fresh fish. Only then will I pick up my recipe book for inspiration on how to cook them well. I have written this book with this way of planning meals in mind, putting vegetables first.

I like to feel good about the food I eat, and so I cook with ingredients that have been ethically sourced. It's a big driving force for me to buy food in as conscious a way as possible. But how do we decide for ourselves what's ethical and what's not? At my restaurant, Poco, we've drawn up a manifesto so that we and—importantly—our customers know where we stand. I've brought our ethos to this book.

I like to have a connection to where my food comes from, even if it's just talking to a market stall-holder or chatting to a fishmonger to find out how the fish was caught. This helps me to value the food I'm eating and respect its origins. If you do the same, you'll even pick up the occasional bargain . . .

It's a no-brainer that cooking with natural foods means a healthier body and a healthier planet. Farming naturally, without the use of pesticides and fertilizers, helps our eco-system become more diverse, more fertile, and more healthy.

In order to reduce my impact on the planet, I cook with local ingredients. You will only find a minimal amount of imported produce in these recipes. I use key whole foods that might not already have their own spot on your kitchen shelf, but which I hope will in future, such as spelt flour, rapadura—a raw sugar that contains all the molasses and nutrients—and raw (not heat-treated) local honey. You can buy these in most grocery store or in health food stores.

Fortunately it is these seasonal, local, whole, and organic foods that taste the best, too. The best chefs cook with them, and for good reason. If we buy and value these ingredients and use them economically then good food doesn't have to cost the earth.

Love and cook with wild abandon.

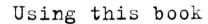

Using this book

Every chapter explores six or seven seasonal "hero" ingredients that are readily available in our markets. Each ingredient is represented first by three super-simple yet favorite preparations of mine that you can make using a few ingredients from your larder. If you have time to go to the market—or happen to have other seasonal ingredients available—you can also pick from three world-inspired seasonal recipes that include that already-prepared simple dish.

The recipes in this book are ideas and starting points. So feel free to use what ingredients you have and make up your own versions. When making my socca pizza, for example, substitute the asparagus topping for any other seasonal veggies in your refrigerator that you think might work well, grilled or sautéed. And consider removing sugar from the recipes, or replacing it with honey, if you want.

I've also given clear tips and ideas for how to turn leftovers from the recipes into other delicious meals, and explained how they should be stored to keep them at their best and avoid waste.

Eat well, waste nothing

We all hate waste. According to the Government-funded waste and resources action program, households throw away up to 40 percent of all the food they buy, moving it straight from the refrigerator to the trash without it ever reaching the table.

I've written tips on every recipe to help make the most of the food we buy. We can easily reduce the waste in our own kitchens and, by doing so, save not only our resources but also a little extra money to buy higher welfare meat and better quality veggies.

I try my best to reduce waste. But somehow there's always something I miss that ends up in the compost. The carrot that gets too wrinkly, the herbs that wilt, or leftovers I just didn't feel like eating until it was too late. Here are a few ideas that we use in my restaurant and at home to help keep our waste to a minimum:

- Be creative! Search around in the refrigerator or cupboards, find what needs using up, then put a meal together that uses those ingredients. Keep it simple and you can't go wrong.

- Shop wisely. Before you go shopping, "stock take," and make a list of what you already have so that you can build it into your week's meals. Don't be fooled into purchasing bulk buys that you will never eat. Buy vegetables and meat loose from the market, in smaller quantities. Root veg, and hardy squash, onions, and garlic keep for longer, so you can buy lots at the same time, but be wary when it comes to herbs, soft fruits, salad, and leafy greens, and buy in smaller quantities.

- Portion sizes. Cook just enough, but, if you cook too much, keep it for lunch the next day, or freeze portions to use later.

- Thrift. Remember what your grandma taught you! Use everything. Eat leftovers. Don't peel veg; the goodness is in the skin. There's plenty of tips about what to do with all sorts of leftovers in this book.

- Sell/Use by dates. These are there to ensure food gets to our houses in tip-top condition. If low-risk foods such as vegetables, yogurt, and cheeses pass their "use by" date, *don't throw them away before checking them*. Smell the food and check for mold. If it smells OK, it probably is OK. Even meat will be OK after its "use by" date if kept in the correct conditions.

- Store food correctly. As a rule, keep fresh fruit and veg in the refrigerator at 37 to 39°F [3 to 4°C]. Store root veg in a dark cupboard. Keep bananas in a separate bowl, unless you want to ripen other fruit. Make the most of your freezer. It's great for saving food when you don't have time to cook or eat it.

- Ration plastics. Look for alternatives to food sold in packaging, and use washed plastic bags instead of plastic wrap. And wash and reuse freezer bags, too. Avoid foil and use pots and pans with lids instead. If you have to use foil, recycle it.

Seasonality

I feel blessed each month as new ingredients ripen and appear in the market. Summer offers us a huge variety of delicious berries, soft fruits, beans, and Mediterranean vegetables. As fall nears, our fields bulge with an abundance of fruits and vegetables to forage, pot, jar, and can for the cold months ahead. Even winter has a wealth of fresh ingredients, from roots and tubers to fresh curly kales. Completing the cycle as the sun begins to shine again, spring brings us the delicacies of asparagus, perky radishes, and rhubarb to wake up our taste buds after a long winter of comfort food.

Seasonal ingredients and quality go hand in hand. Fruits and vegetables that are picked at their peak not only taste better but also use fewer resources to grow and are often transported much shorter distances to your table. The flavor and texture of a juicy local tomato in summer is almost completely incomparable to that of an imported winter tomato, yet both fetch a similar price. By using the seasonal fruit and vegetables in this book as a shopping list for the appropriate months, you will effortlessly improve the quality of your food while decreasing the resources needed to produce that food. Buying seasonal produce from your local stores will also help support your community and its farmers.

Big grocery stores ignore the seasons, giving us a generic list of ingredients available all year round. This puts massive pressure on our resources and needlessly neglects the bounty of ingredients that we have on our doorstep. With a select choice of the best local, seasonal ingredients you will naturally become a more creative cook, and with these simple recipes you will make incredibly delicious meals.

Meat

When buying meat, I tend to experiment with the cheaper cuts. I buy local pasture fed meat and make sure it is the best quality I can afford. A fillet steak is tender, but a rump has more flavor, while an ox cheek cooked long and slow, as in the recipe on page 121, will melt in your mouth. Even though these cuts have been popularized by chefs, they still come at a more affordable price.

The best thing you can do to reduce your carbon footprint is *eat less meat*. The amount of grain it takes to feed a cow and produce one steak is disproportionate to the number of meals that grain would provide. If in doubt, organic is a good certification to go by, as it not only ensures your meat will be free from hormones and high doses of antibiotics, but is also a general indication of higher welfare, as it requires that animals are genuinely free-range.

Fish

These days fish stocks are depleted and a lot of species are endangered. We need to be *very* careful which fish we are buying as it is an ever-changing situation. Some fishmongers who advertise themselves as "sustainable" still sell endangered species. It's up to us to do the research and make the decisions on what fish we buy. I buy fish that is in season and caught locally. Refer to an online guide such as FishWatch (www.fishwatch.gov) to make sure you're buying fish from sustainable stocks.

Whole foods

Whole foods are downright delicious. Whole grains and pulses, vegetables, a crusty loaf of brown bread, or whole grain pasta have twice the flavor of their bland, processed counterparts. Flavor is what I look for in my cooking and whole foods always deliver. Of course we're also doing our well-being a massive favor, as whole foods are far more nutritionally rewarding. Heavily processed ingredients, or "the white stuff"—rice, sugar, pasta, and flour—contain simple carbohydrates that break down into simple sugars that we just don't need. It's not that whole foods are the only option, just that they are something I'd rather eat more of . . . and I feel better for it, too. The Fava bean and lamb pilaf with seasoned yogurt (see page 67) is a prime example of just how good whole grain rice can be. It carries the rich, savory, spicy flavors perfectly. Spelt flour, which I use as a replacement for wheat flour in most recipes, is easy to work with and tastes delicious. Spelt makes amazing bread, due to its high protein content, as well as great pastry: check out the Spinach and smoked fish tart on page 151.

Growing your own, and the compost monster!

You don't need a garden to grow a few pots of herbs and vegetables. It takes little effort and it's so rewarding. You can grow anywhere, on windowsills, on the porch, or on the driveway. Start with herbs, as they can be so expensive to buy, and take up little room. Radishes are fun to grow in spring as they take just three or four weeks from seed. Chard and kale are easy to grow all year round and just keep giving. Zucchini are prolific, grow well in pots, and give you the benefit of being able to eat their stems and flowers. It's also nice to grow things that you can't easily buy, such as purple basil, or heirloom varieties of carrots and tomatoes. Try upcycling empty egg boxes into planters for seedlings, or using old cans and bottles for pots.

If you're going to grow your own, it is worth starting a compost pile to give free, nourishing fertilizer. You can buy compost bins, or make one out of a regular bin by drilling plenty of holes in it. Feed it with a mixture of green and brown natural waste. The bulk of the compost needs to be brown: twigs, paper, cardboard, bread, egg shells, tea, and coffee. Then add green matter from fruit, veg, and leaves. Avoid adding meat, fish, and dairy as they attract animals. Mix the compost every few weeks with a garden fork to aerate and keep it healthy. I keep two composters (see the photo on page 176), so that when one is ready I can be working on the next. After about six months, your compost should be ready to start mixing into your soil. Get growing!

Cook Natural . . .

. . . means to me using whole, minimally-processed, ripe, local, seasonal food. In other words, food of the very best quality.

I firmly believe we all really do care about where our food comes from, whether we're concerned about the excessive use of chemicals, animal welfare, food-miles and waste, taste and quality, or all of the above.

As we all know, in the real world where money is tight and there's a grocery store on every corner, shopping responsibly can feel like an uphill battle. However, by committing a little time to understanding the principles of seasonal food and cooking, we could all eat more organic ingredients, enjoy farmers' markets, and support local suppliers *without spending more*. Over the years my morals have wavered at times—by not always buying local or free-range—in order to keep things ticking over and costs down. But I have now learned that you can keep to a strict budget while using exceptionally high-quality products. All it takes is a little thrift, a seasonal approach, and the use of cheaper cuts. Now I simply won't use an ingredient if it doesn't match my principles; I will always find another route or recipe to replace it . . . and keep to my budget, too. This book is about how to eat consciously. How to empower our food choices and enrich our diets, while keeping peace of mind about everything that we cook.

Most of all, this book is a celebration of our delicious seasonal and local foods—those that are abundant, not rare—drawing on age-old culinary wisdom with recipes that make use of every last bit of an ingredient and waste nothing.

Cook with local whole foods and vegetables, be inspired by world recipes and traditions.

Eat the best food you can.

EATING SPRING

artichokes

asparagus

broccoli

blood oranges, navel oranges, and lemons

carrots

cauliflowers

leeks

mushrooms (cultivated)

new potatoes

radishes

rhubarb

salad leaves

~~scallions~~

spinach

spring cabbages

watercress

Eating
ASPARAGUS

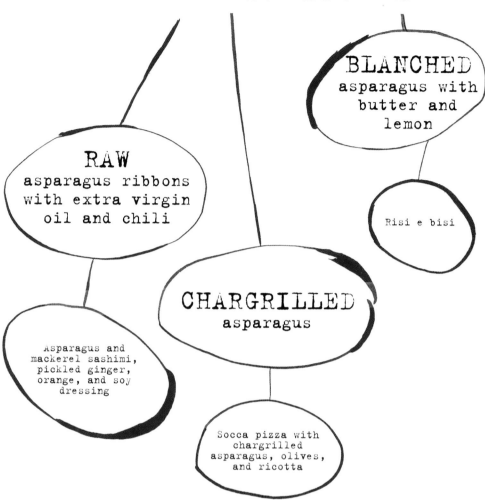

BLANCHED
asparagus with
butter and
lemon

Risi e bisi

RAW
asparagus ribbons
with extra virgin
oil and chili

Asparagus and
mackerel sashimi,
pickled ginger,
orange, and soy
dressing

CHARGRILLED
asparagus

Socca pizza with
chargrilled
asparagus, olives,
and ricotta

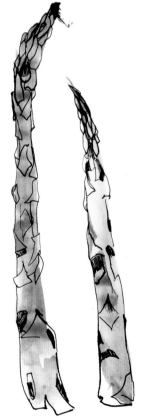

April to June Ready, set, go . . . when the asparagus season starts, make sure you're the first to the store, as you've only got six weeks to enjoy this tender and flavorsome treat. Steam, boil, stir-fry, barbecue, or just eat it raw, but make sure it's sitting in pride of place on your table, preferably with a big pot of aïoli (see page 81) next to it for dipping. The important thing to remember when cooking asparagus is that the stalks take just a minute or two to cook and should be devoured just as quickly.

Asparagus has a distinctive but delicate stand-alone flavor that doesn't need any complication; this is a vegetable to cook simply. It is best eaten as fresh as possible, so buy as local as you can. If the cut ends look dry, trim them off and keep your stalks fresh by standing them in a cup of water in the refrigerator.

If the asparagus is on the sturdy side, peel the thickest ends to remove any tough skin. Then cut off the bottom ¾ to 1 in [2 to 3 cm] of the stalk and take a bite where you cut at the base of the spear to test the texture . . . now decide whether to cut off any more. The woody part can be added to soup or stock. Usually, chefs suggest that you bend the stalk to see where it snaps, only keeping the very tender tops. I don't, because this method wastes a great deal of asparagus that I'd rather have on my plate!

Blanched asparagus with butter and lemon

So simple and so delicious. The trick here is to use lots of water, so its temperature doesn't drop too much when you add the asparagus. Olive oil is just as good with the spears as butter, if you prefer. Serves 2 as a side dish or appetizer.

12 asparagus spears, knob of butter, squeeze of lemon

Bring a large pan of salted water to a boil. Chop off the bottom ¾ to 1 in [2 to 3 cm] or so of the woody ends of the asparagus spears (see opposite) and save them to add to a stock or a soup. When the water is at a rolling boil, drop in the asparagus. Leave two to three minutes, then drain and return the stalks to the pan with the butter and lemon juice, a pinch of pepper, and some salt if you think it needs it. Turn the stalks in the butter and lemon and serve immediately.

MORE BLANCHED ASPARAGUS . . . AND LEFTOVERS
With a soft-boiled egg, makes a really fabulous and healthy breakfast.

Open lasagne. Preheat the oven to 375°F [190°C]. Chop leftover Blanched asparagus with butter and lemon into rough lengths and mix into a little ricotta. Place between two precooked lasagne sheets, grate parmesan over the top, and put in the hot oven 10 minutes. Serves 1.

Risi e bisi

An asparagus version of a Venetian soup traditionally made with rice and peas (risi e bisi). It's a bit like a loose risotto and very warming. You can add lardoons of pancetta or bacon if you like, but I've gone for a vegetarian recipe. Serves 4 as an appetizer.

1 quantity Blanched asparagus with butter and lemon, chopped into ¾ to 1 in [2 to 3 cm] pieces on the diagonal
1 onion, finely chopped (add the skin to the stock)
4 garlic cloves, roughly chopped
Dash of light olive oil
1 cup [200 g] short-grain brown rice (from health food stores), or regular risotto rice
14 oz [400 g] fresh peas, unpodded weight (add the pods to the stock), or 3½ oz [100 g] frozen peas
A few sprigs herbs (I used oregano, mint, and chives), finely chopped
A little grated parmesan, as much as you like
Knob of butter
Extra virgin olive oil (optional)
Lemon wedges

For the stock
1 carrot, grated
1 onion, grated
1 leek, finely chopped
Any other veg you need to use up!

Make the stock: put the vegetables in a saucepan with 5½ cups [1.3 L] of water. Bring to a boil with the vegetable trimmings and pea pods, then reduce the heat to a simmer 30 minutes. Strain, then return the stock to the pan over low heat.

In a separate saucepan, sauté the onion and garlic in the light olive oil with a pinch of salt over gentle heat 5 to 10 minutes, until soft. Tip in the rice and fry another 2 minutes. Pour over the hot stock and bring to a gentle simmer. Cook about 25 minutes (15 minutes if using white rice), stirring regularly, until the rice is just cooked but still firm. Add extra water if necessary; this should have a soup-like consistency.

Add the asparagus, peas, herbs, parmesan, and butter. Stir and simmer 3 minutes, then taste and adjust the levels of cheese and seasoning. Serve in warmed bowls with more parmesan on top. I like to drizzle on extra virgin olive oil, too, and offer lemon wedges.

STORAGE Keep any leftover blanched asparagus or risi e bisi in sealed containers in the refrigerator up to 3 days. The asparagus is best returned to room temperature to serve, or reheat it gently in a sauté pan if you prefer. When you reheat the soup, it will thicken into a risotto, as the rice will have drunk up the liquid. Add a little extra parmesan to serve.

Chargrilled asparagus

Sweet asparagus is an excellent candidate for the charred, bitter magic worked by the grill. It is best cooked on a charcoal barbecue, otherwise a griddle pan will be fine. Always use lumpwood charcoal for cooking, as it is cleaner and gives a much better flavor. (Briquettes and instant charcoal contain flammable chemicals that taint the food.) Serves 1 as a side dish; simply scale up the amounts to serve more.

6 asparagus spears, light olive oil

Light the barbecue and allow the coals to turn white hot and then to cool a little, or heat a griddle pan over high heat. Chop off the bottom ¾ to 1 in [2 to 3 cm] or so of the woody ends of the asparagus spears (see page 12) and save them to add to a stock or soup. Roll the spears in the light olive oil, salt, and pepper, then place on the heat. Allow to blacken just slightly, then turn to char the other sides. Serve immediately.

MORE CHARGRILLED ASPARAGUS . . .
AND LEFTOVERS
With romesco sauce (see page 37). Wonderful.

Fattoush with socca. Socca is gluten-free and can be used to replace bread, so try adding it to Fattoush (see page 88) instead of pitta or flatbread, for a gluten-free version.

Socca pizza with chargrilled asparagus, olives, and ricotta

Discovering socca pizza was a recent revelation in my kitchen. I love pizza, but don't want to eat gluten and wheat every day. Socca pizza is made with chickpea flour, is simple to cook, and has a satisfying, nutty flavor that goes well with these toppings. But play around with the socca bases, adding your own favorite toppings. Serves 2 as an appetizer.

For the toppings
1 quantity Chargrilled asparagus,
  bases of the stalks finely chopped
6 to 8 halves of oven-dried tomatoes (see recipe method),
  or sun-dried tomatoes
6 Greek olives, pitted
3½ oz [100 g] ricotta
Handful basil leaves

For the base
1⅔ cups [200 g] chickpea (gram) flour
1 Tbsp extra virgin olive oil
1 tsp dried oregano or herbes de Provence
Glug of light olive oil, plus more for the tomatoes

To oven-dry tomatoes, preheat the oven to 225°F [110°C]. Halve as many tomatoes as you have available and scoop out and compost the seeds. Place the tomatoes, cut-sides down, on a wire cooling rack, with a baking sheet underneath to catch drips. Cook in the oven 3 to 5 hours. If you are using the oven to dry tomatoes, then make the most of it and fill it up with other fruits or vegetables that are good dried. Try halved apricots, slices of apple, or mango.

To make the socca base, mix the chickpea flour, extra virgin oil, dried herbs, and salt and pepper together with 14 Tbsp [250 ml] of water, whisking until you have a smooth batter. Add a little more water if necessary. Preheat a grill on its highest setting.

Heat a large ovenproof skillet with a little light olive oil. Pour in the batter and swivel the pan to spread it out like a thin pancake. Cook over medium heat until golden brown, then flip carefully with a spatula and cook until golden brown and a little crispy.

Place on the toppings (except the basil) and put under the hot grill 5 minutes, until it's hot and bubbling. Season, tear over the basil, and serve.

STORAGE Chargrilled asparagus will keep in a sealed container in the refrigerator up to 3 days. Return it to room temperature to serve as a cold side dish or part of a salad. The pizza keeps in the refrigerator 4 days and is great as a cold snack, but is best fresh and hot. Oven-dried tomatoes will keep under a layer of olive oil in a sterilized jar 6 months.

Raw asparagus ribbons with extra virgin oil and chili

I like to eat as much raw food as possible, as it keeps me feeling light and healthy. Asparagus is fantastic eaten raw, so make the most of it. Serves 1 to 2 as a side salad.

4 asparagus spears, extra virgin olive oil, chili flakes

Rinse the asparagus. Using a vegetable peeler, peel off ribbons of asparagus until you're left with just the woody end (save this for a stock or soup). The last tender bit of asparagus is difficult to peel into a ribbon, so finely chop it with a knife. Dress the ribbons and finely chopped asparagus with a little extra virgin oil and season with salt and a dusting of chili flakes, to taste.

MORE RAW ASPARAGUS . . . AND LEFTOVERS
With mozzarella, apricots, and a herb dressing.
Mix Raw asparagus ribbons with extra virgin oil and chili with a ball of ripped mozzarella and 3 torn apricots. Chop a few sprigs of any soft herbs, put in a small bowl, season, and add a little extra virgin oil and some capers if you have them. Toss with the salad, arrange on plates, and serve. Serves 2 as a light lunch.

With soft-boiled eggs, anchovies, and sumac.
Soft-boil two eggs as you like them, let cool, then chop into quarters and arrange on a plate with a few anchovies and 1 quantity Raw asparagus ribbons with extra virgin oil and chili. Sprinkle with sumac, a little more extra virgin oil and chili, to taste, and salt and pepper. Serves 1.

Asparagus and mackerel sashimi, pickled ginger, orange, and soy dressing

Tell your fishmonger that you are making sashimi and ask for the freshest fish. Get it filleted, pin-boned, and skinned, so that it's ready to use. Serves 2 as an appetizer.

1 quantity Raw asparagus ribbons with extra virgin oil and chili
1 orange
2 mackerel fillets, skinned and pin-boned
Pinch pickled ginger

For the dressing
1 Tbsp tamari or soy sauce
1 tsp raw local honey
Wasabi, to taste

First make the dressing. Mix all the ingredients and taste, adding more wasabi if you like it hot.

Peel the orange with a knife, removing the pith and skin, then slice it into rounds, flicking out any seeds you find as you go.

Cut the mackerel fillets lengthwise, down either side of the spine, discarding the central piece with any remaining pin-bones that may be lurking there. Now cut each half into 1½ in [4 cm] lengths.

Arrange the fish, orange, and asparagus ribbons on the plates. Dress each piece of fish with a little of the dressing, then dress the rest of the ingredients sparingly. Scatter with pickled ginger.

STORAGE Eat the raw asparagus ribbons immediately. The sashimi dish should also be eaten straightaway, but keeps in a sealed container in the refrigerator up to a day if necessary. Return to room temperature to serve.

COOK NATURAL Be conscious of how fish was caught and don't be afraid to ask the fishmonger. If he or she doesn't know, it's a bad sign. Always check fish has clear eyes and skin. Take a sniff: it should smell fresh and of the sea. Trust your instincts and go for the freshest fish available, even if it means going home with a different species from the one you came to buy.

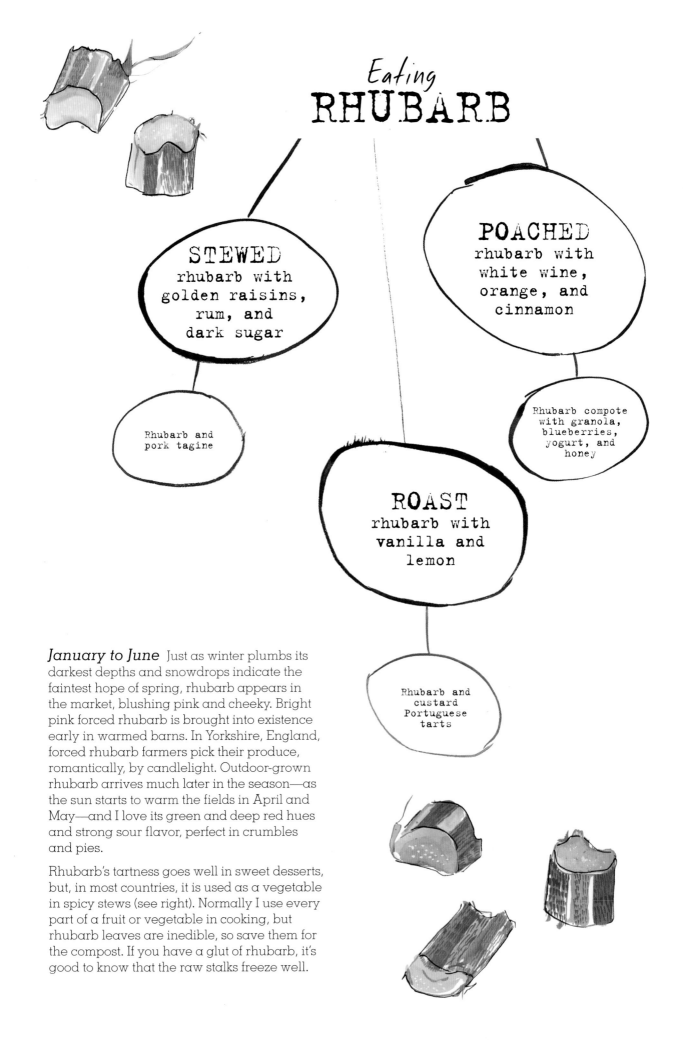

Eating RHUBARB

STEWED
rhubarb with golden raisins, rum, and dark sugar

Rhubarb and pork tagine

POACHED
rhubarb with white wine, orange, and cinnamon

Rhubarb compote with granola, blueberries, yogurt, and honey

ROAST
rhubarb with vanilla and lemon

Rhubarb and custard Portuguese tarts

January to June Just as winter plumbs its darkest depths and snowdrops indicate the faintest hope of spring, rhubarb appears in the market, blushing pink and cheeky. Bright pink forced rhubarb is brought into existence early in warmed barns. In Yorkshire, England, forced rhubarb farmers pick their produce, romantically, by candlelight. Outdoor-grown rhubarb arrives much later in the season—as the sun starts to warm the fields in April and May—and I love its green and deep red hues and strong sour flavor, perfect in crumbles and pies.

Rhubarb's tartness goes well in sweet desserts, but, in most countries, it is used as a vegetable in spicy stews (see right). Normally I use every part of a fruit or vegetable in cooking, but rhubarb leaves are inedible, so save them for the compost. If you have a glut of rhubarb, it's good to know that the raw stalks freeze well.

Stewed rhubarb with golden raisins, rum, and dark sugar

Stewing is the simplest way to make rhubarb taste wonderful. I like to keep a pot of this in the refrigerator in springtime, to eat with yogurt as a light dessert. It's very easy to turn into a sweet chutney, too (see below). Serves 4 as an element of dessert or breakfast.

7 oz [200 g] rhubarb, splash of rum, ¾ cup [75 g] dark muscovado sugar, scattering of golden raisins

Wash the rhubarb, then cut it into irregular pieces. Put into a small saucepan with the rum, sugar, and golden raisins. Put the lid on and bring to a gentle simmer, then cover and stir occasionally. After 5 to 10 minutes, the rhubarb will soften. Remove from the heat.

MORE STEWED RHUBARB . . . AND LEFTOVERS
Chutney. If you have an abundance of rhubarb, making chutney is the best and tastiest thing you can do. When boiling 1 quantity Stewed rhubarb with golden raisins, rum, and dark sugar, add a thumb of ginger root, grated, 1 small finely chopped onion, 3 oz [80 ml] cider vinegar, 1 tsp ground coriander, and a generous pinch of salt. Boil 5 minutes, then pot into a hot sterilized 1⅛ lb [500 g] jar (see page 52) while still hot. Seal. Makes about one 1⅛ lb [500 g] jar.

Pork and rhubarb puff pie. Preheat the oven to 350°F [180°C]. Put leftover Rhubarb and pork tagine into a suitably sized ovenproof dish and top with Rough puff pastry (see page 82). Bake in the hot oven 20 to 25 minutes.

Rhubarb and pork tagine

Sour rhubarb goes really well with sweet pork and is nice slowly cooked in a tagine. The rich sauce works well with a side of steamed bulgar wheat or couscous (see page 104). Serves 4.

1 quantity Stewed rhubarb with golden raisins, rum, and dark sugar
14 oz [400 g] pork shoulder, chopped into chunks
Good glug light olive oil
3 onions, sliced
4 garlic cloves, roughly chopped
2 tsp ground coriander
14 Tbsp [200 ml] white wine
2 turnips (or potatoes), cut into wedges
6 sprigs cilantro, stalks finely chopped, leaves roughly chopped

Find a large saucepan that has a lid. Sear the pork in the light olive oil in small batches, allowing it to brown and caramelize on each side. Take your time with this, as it will give the tagine plenty of extra flavor. If you crowd the pan it will lose temperature and stew the meat, making it difficult to caramelize the edges and sweeten the flavor. Remove the pork from the pan with a slotted spoon, leaving the fat, then repeat to cook the rest of the meat.

Cook the onions slowly in the pork fat left in the pan, with the garlic and ground coriander, 10 minutes, until really soft. Add the wine and bring to a boil, scraping all the sticky bits from the base of the pan.

Return the pork to the saucepan with the rhubarb and turnips or potatoes. Put the lid on and reduce the heat to its lowest. Cook 1½ hours, until the pork is tender. Taste and adjust the seasoning, then serve strewn with the cilantro leaves.

STORAGE Stewed rhubarb will keep 4 days in a sealed container in the refrigerator. Return to room temperature before serving. Tagines, like stews, get better with age. Consider cooking the tagine the day before you want it, for a mellower flavor. It will keep 4 days in a sealed container in the refrigerator. Reheat it gently on the stovetop until hot right through.

COOK NATURAL Herb stalks taste delicious and should be eaten whenever possible. They are more flavorful than the leaves, but tougher, so they need to be finely chopped. If you have any particularly tough stalks, you can save them to add to stocks instead.

Poached rhubarb with orange, and cinnamon

Reduce the cooking liquor until it's a delicious thick syrup, then pour it back over the rhubarb, or save it to pour over your oatmeal or yogurt. Serves 4 as an element of dessert or breakfast.

14 Tbsp [200 ml] just-squeezed orange juice (about 3 oranges), 1½ cups [300 g] rapadura or raw cane sugar, 1 cinnamon stick, 10½ oz [300 g] rhubarb

Bring the orange juice and sugar to a boil. Add the cinnamon, peel off a piece of orange zest with a vegetable peeler, and add that, too. Cut the rhubarb into ¾ to 1 in [2 to 3 cm] long pieces. Drop it into the poaching liquor and simmer 5 minutes. Check to see if it's cooked by lifting a piece out of the liquid and pressing: it should feel soft. If it's still hard, cook another minute or so. Remove all the rhubarb from the syrup with a slotted spoon and let cool.

MORE POACHED RHUBARB . . . AND LEFTOVERS
Rhubarb granola crumble. Preheat the oven to 340°F [170°C]. Fill an ovenproof dish with Poached rhubarb with white wine, orange, and cinnamon. Cover with a thin layer of Granola (see right). Bake 15 minutes, or until hot right through. Serve with pudding or cream. Serves 4.

Crème brûlée. Preheat the oven to 325°F [160°C]. Whisk 2 eggs with 14 Tbsp [200 ml] whole milk, 14 Tbsp [200 ml] heavy cream, 5 Tbsp [75 g] rapadura or raw cane sugar, and the seeds of a vanilla pod. Put a spoon of poached rhubarb in the bottom of each of four ramekins, then top with the pudding mixture. Put them in a deep tray and pour boiling water to come two-thirds of the way up the side of the ramekins. Put into the hot oven 35 minutes, or until just set when wobbled. Remove from the water, let cool, then refrigerate 2 or 3 hours. Make a caramel by heating ½ cup [100 g] raw cane sugar in a dry pan. When it begins to bubble and has melted, carefully pour a little over each ramekin, then allow to set. If you own a blowtorch you could scorch a thin layer of sugar on top instead, but the caramel method is an easier way to get a good crunchy caramel topping without special kit. Makes 4.

Rhubarb compote with granola, blueberries, yogurt, and honey

A delicious and healthy breakfast. If you're in a rush, blend the rhubarb into a smoothie with a little orange juice, the yogurt, blueberries, and honey instead. The compote can be changed from season to season as each fruit becomes available, from strawberries to pears. The compote serves 4, but the granola makes enough for 10, so feel free to double up the compote recipe if you've got a crowd coming for brunch.

For the compote and to serve
1 quantity Poached rhubarb with white wine, orange, and cinnamon
2⅛ cups [500 ml] pot live natural yogurt
Blueberries, as many as you like
Raw local honey, to taste

For the granola
2½ cups [200 g] whole oats
¾ cup [100 g] seeds, such as sunflower, sesame, and pumpkin
1 cup [100 g] nuts, such as walnuts, almonds, and hazelnuts
2 tsp vanilla extract
6 Tbsp raw local honey or maple syrup
3 Tbsp flavorless vegetable oil
1¾ oz [50 g] dates, roughly chopped
1¾ oz [50 g] dried figs, roughly chopped
1¾ oz [50 g] goji berries or raisins

Preheat the oven to 350°F [180°C]. Put all the granola ingredients except the fruits into a bowl and massage the honey or syrup and oil into everything. Scatter evenly over a baking sheet and put into the oven 20 to 25 minutes. Check halfway and scrape any cooked brown bits from the edges to the center.

When the granola starts to color a little and firm up, add the fruit and return to the oven 5 minutes. Let cool.

Fill a breakfast bowl with a few spoons of thick yogurt and a couple of spoons of the rhubarb. Scatter with blueberries and a good helping of granola. Drizzle with honey and serve.

STORAGE The granola, once cooled, will keep in an airtight jar for months. The poached rhubarb will keep 4 days in a sealed container in the refrigerator. Return it to room temperature to serve.

Roast rhubarb with vanilla and lemon

This is my favorite way to cook rhubarb. It holds its shape perfectly, is blushed with pink, and has a sugary glaze. I like to roast rhubarb for fools, frangipane, pannacotta, and as a side dish to serve with roast pork. Serves 4.

12¼ oz [350 g] rhubarb, 5 Tbsp [75 g] rapadura or raw cane sugar, a few drops of vanilla extract, juice of ½ lemon

Preheat the oven to 350°F [180°C]. Wash the rhubarb, then cut it into 1 to 2 in [2.5 to 5 cm] pieces. Spread them out on a baking sheet. Sprinkle with the sugar, vanilla, and lemon juice. Cover with foil and put into the oven 10 minutes. Remove the foil and check the rhubarb is cooked by gently pressing a piece; it should be just soft. Eat as it is, with ice cream, or make into a fool (see below).

MORE ROAST RHUBARB . . . AND LEFTOVERS
Rhubarb bellini. Keep some of the syrup from the Roast rhubarb with vanilla and lemon to make a delicious cocktail. Put 1 Tbsp of the syrup in a fluted glass and top up with cava or prosecco. Stir lightly and serve. Makes 1.

Rhubarb fool. Whisk 3½ Tbsp [50 ml] heavy cream to soft peaks. Carefully fold in 7 Tbsp [100 ml] thick live natural yogurt, then ½ quantity Roast rhubarb with vanilla and lemon. Spoon into glasses. Makes 4.

Rhubarb and pudding Portuguese tarts

These are one of my favorite treats, gobbled up with an espresso at breakfast. The sweet-and-sourness of the roast rhubarb takes this classic tart to another level. Makes about 12.

1 quantity Roast rhubarb with vanilla and lemon
1¼ cups [300 ml] whole milk
2 pieces unwaxed lemon zest, removed with a vegetable peeler
Seeds of 1 vanilla pod, or 1 tsp vanilla extract
3 eggs
¾ cup [160 g] rapadura or raw cane sugar
1 Tbsp plain or spelt flour
½ quantity (about 7 oz [200 g]) Rough puff pastry (see page 82)

Preheat the oven to its highest setting. Pour the milk into a saucepan over medium heat with the lemon zest and vanilla. Bring to a boil, then remove from the heat. Meanwhile, beat the eggs with the sugar in a large bowl. Put the flour in a small bowl or cup.

Add 1 Tbsp of the hot milk to the flour and mix it up to make a smooth paste. Pour the rest of the milk over the egg mixture, whisking constantly to stop it scrambling, then whisk in the flour paste. Let cool a little, then remove the lemon zest.

Roll out the pastry and cut out about 12 squares that fit into a muffin tray with a slight overhang when pressed to the bottom. (Freeze any leftover pastry, or make Off-cut pastry biscuits, see page 116.) Press all the pastry squares into the muffin tray and place a couple of sticks of roast rhubarb in each, with a little drizzle of its roasting syrup. Fill with the pudding two-thirds full.

Put in the oven 10 to 12 minutes until the pudding is bubbling and the pastry dark brown. Remove and let cool on a rack. Best eaten as soon as they are cold.

STORAGE Both the roast rhubarb and the tarts will keep in a sealed container in the refrigerator 4 days. Return both to room temperature before serving.

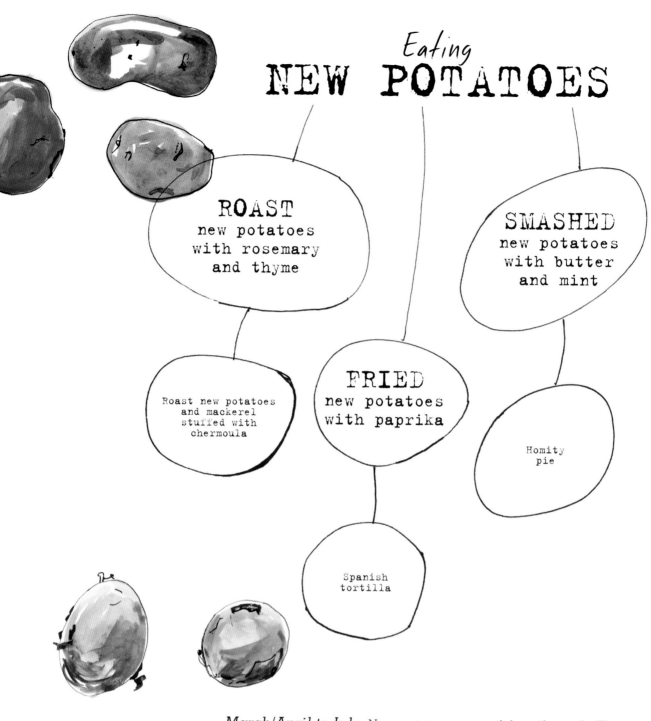

Eating
NEW POTATOES

ROAST
new potatoes
with rosemary
and thyme

SMASHED
new potatoes
with butter
and mint

Roast new potatoes
and mackerel
stuffed with
chermoula

FRIED
new potatoes
with paprika

Homity
pie

Spanish
tortilla

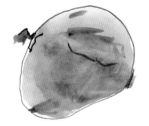

March/April to July New potatoes are a gift from the gods. The Inca gods of Peru, in fact. Potatoes were first cultivated 8,000 years ago around Lake Titicaca. New potatoes, the earliest to harvest in the year, are so delicious that all they need is a quick boil 10 minutes or so, until tender, then an anointing with a dash of extra virgin oil or a knob of butter and a sprig of mint. They also roast well (see page 27), making a good alternative to the common roast potato and with less waste (and prep work), too. Don't peel new potatoes; all the goodness is in or just under the skin.

The trick with buying a good new potato is to find them fresh and dirty; they will be full of flavor with a flaky skin. They keep much better when cloaked in dirt, protecting them both from the light and from easy bruising. Store them in a cool, dark place in a kitchen cupboard, vegetable rack, or larder, with the soil still on them.

Fried new potatoes with paprika

The perfect fried potato should be soft on the inside but crisp, savory, and flavorful on the outside. Serves 2 as a side dish.

12¼ oz [350 g] new potatoes, glug of light olive oil, sweet paprika

Scrub the potatoes to remove any dirt, then cut any large ones in half so all the pieces are roughly the same size. Bring to a boil in a saucepan of salted water, then reduce the heat and simmer 8 to 10 minutes, until just soft. Check by pushing a butter knife into a potato; if it goes in without too much resistance, they are ready. Be careful not to let them get too soft, otherwise they will fall apart during frying. Drain and cool, then dry, cut into cubes, and fry in the oil over medium-high heat 10 minutes. Keep turning to ensure a good all-round golden, crisp skin. When ready, sprinkle with paprika and salt.

MORE FRIED NEW POTATOES . . . AND LEFTOVERS
Patatas bravas. Start this Spanish classic by making a simple tomato sauce: finely chop 1 onion, 1 garlic clove, and 1 celery stick and fry in light olive oil until soft. Add a 14 oz [400 g] can of tomatoes and a sprinkle of cayenne pepper. Season and simmer 10 minutes, then serve over Fried new potatoes with paprika. Serves 2 as part of a mixed tapas.

Bombay potatoes. Fry a sliced onion with 2 finely chopped garlic cloves in a knob of butter. Add 2 tsp garam masala and 1 tsp turmeric, then the Fried new potatoes with paprika and a scattering of frozen peas. Pour in a splash of water and scrape any sticky bits from the base of the pan. Serves 2 as a side dish.

Spanish tortilla

A simple dish, yet so delicious when made with care. Everyone has their own way of making tortilla. This version was taught to me by an outrageously good chef, my friend Marianna. I like it best a little soft in the middle; it has the most wonderful creamy texture. Serves 4 as a generous lunch.

1 quantity Fried new potatoes
  with paprika
2 onions, sliced
Light olive oil
2 garlic cloves, roughly chopped
4 eggs, lightly beaten

Slowly sauté the onions 15 to 20 minutes in light olive oil until they are very soft. Add the garlic and fry another 2 minutes. Add the onions to the potatoes and let it all cool. Now add the eggs and mix, crushing the potatoes a little as you do so. Season with salt and pepper. Now taste a little of the mixture . . . scary, I know, but worth it to adjust the seasoning and make it perfect.

Heat a deep 6 to 8 in [15 to 20 cm] skillet with a good splash more light olive oil. When the oil begins to smoke, pour in the egg mixture; be careful, it may spit. Swivel the pan from side to side with the handle so it doesn't stick. You should see the egg moving independently from the pan itself.

Reduce the heat to its lowest and cook 4 or 5 minutes. Place your finger in the middle and feel how far through the egg is cooked, too. When it is cooked halfway through, it is ready to turn. This is the fun part. Put a large plate over the skillet. Using a dish towel and being careful of your hands and arms with the hot oil—and working over the sink in case of any spills—flip on to the plate. This might take a couple of attempts before perfecting.

Return the pan to the heat. Scrape off any bits that may have stuck and add a little more oil. When it's hot, slide the tortilla back into the pan, raw-side down. Shake from side to side again to make sure it's not stuck. Using a wooden spoon, tuck the rough edges underneath to make them rounded, then cook a further 5 minutes. Slide on to a plate and let cool. In Spain, tortilla is served at room temperature—when its flavor shows at its fullest—from the counters of tapas bars, but never chilled.

STORAGE The fried potatoes will keep 3 days in a sealed container in the refrigerator. Reheat in a skillet with a little more oil, if needed, until piping hot. The tortilla will keep well in the refrigerator up to 4 days, but return it to room temperature before eating.

Roast new potatoes with rosemary and thyme

New potatoes roast really well and make a great change from the laborious peeling and unnecessary wastage involved when preparing regular roasties. Serves 4 as a side dish.

1¾ lb [800 g] new potatoes, glug of light olive oil, 3 sprigs rosemary and/or thyme

Preheat the oven to 350°F [180°C]. Scrub the potatoes. Toss them in the oil and herbs with a pinch each of salt and pepper. Roast them in the hot oven 35 to 45 minutes, until golden and soft, turning halfway through. Delicious with any roast meat or fish.

MORE ROAST NEW POTATOES . . . AND LEFTOVERS

Bubble and squeak. Crush and chop cold leftover Roast new potatoes with rosemary and thyme. Fry an onion with any greens you have. Add the potatoes and allow them to crisp up slightly, then fold the mixture over itself, enclosing the crunchy bits inside. Repeat about 10 minutes, until the mixture is hot right through.

Mackerel fish cakes. If you have leftover fish and Roast new potatoes with rosemary and thyme, finely chop the potatoes and pick the fish off the bone. Add chopped parsley and mix with your hands, squashing the ingredients together. Roll into golf ball-sized pieces. Roll the cakes in wholemeal flour, dusting off any excess. Fry in light olive oil 3 minutes each side over medium-high heat, or until hot right through.

Roast new potatoes and mackerel stuffed with chermoula

These salty, flavorsome potatoes work really well with the oily fish and a sweet, zesty chermoula that is full of cilantro leaves. Serves 4.

For the fish and potatoes
1 quantity Roast new potatoes with rosemary and thyme, assembled but not yet cooked
4 mackerel, trimmed and gutted
Light olive oil

For the chermoula
1 red bell pepper, halved and seeded
1 tsp cumin seeds, toasted
1 tsp sweet paprika, plus more for the fish
1 red chili, chopped
2 garlic cloves, chopped
3½ Tbsp [50 g] sprigs cilantro, roughly chopped
2 tsp sprigs of parsley, roughly chopped
Juice of ½ lemon
Extra virgin olive oil

Preheat the oven to 350°F [180°C]. Wash each mackerel well, being sure to remove any of the blood line (the black bit along the spine) that will make it taste bitter. Dry it with paper towels. Put the Roast new potatoes with rosemary and thyme in the oven.

Now make the chermoula. Roast the bell pepper in the oven alongside the potatoes 25 minutes, until soft, then roughly chop. Meanwhile, toast the cumin seeds in a small dry skillet 2 minutes, until smelling aromatic and looking a shade darker. In a mortar and pestle or blender, grind the cumin with the paprika. Add the chili and garlic and grind to a paste. Next, blend in the herbs and roast pepper, then stir in the lemon juice and a good glug of the extra virgin oil. Taste and season with salt and pepper.

Stuff the cavity of each mackerel with a good 2 Tbsp of the chermoula, saving some to dress the potatoes. Put the fish on a baking sheet, drizzle with light olive oil, and season with salt, pepper, and paprika. Cook in the oven alongside the potatoes for the last 15 minutes of their cooking time.

Check the fish is cooked by pressing the meat next to the spine. If it moves off the bone easily, it's cooked. If you're unsure, gently pull the flesh apart with a knife and check it is soft and opaque inside. Serve the fish with the potatoes and extra chermoula on top.

STORAGE Both the fish and the potatoes will keep in sealed containers in the refrigerator 3 days. Reheat both in an oven preheated to 350°F [180°C] until hot right through.

Smashed new potatoes with butter and mint

These take on all the juices from their dressing, packing plenty of flavor. I like them cold with the butter set, as they taste so sweet. Serves 4 as a side dish.

1¾ lb [800 g] new potatoes, 4 sprigs mint, generous knob of butter

Scrub the potatoes to remove any dirt, then cut any large ones in half so all the pieces are roughly the same size. Put in a saucepan and cover with plenty of cold water, adding a generous pinch of salt and three sprigs of mint. Bring to a boil, then reduce the heat and simmer about 15 minutes, or until soft. Test by lightly crushing a potato with the back of a wooden spoon: if it breaks easily, it's ready. Don't let them boil for too long, or you will end up with mash. Remove from the heat and drain. Return to the pan with the butter, the remaining sprig of mint, and generous seasoning. Crush each potato lightly with the back of the wooden spoon and turn them in the butter to coat. Leave to rest with the lid on until you're ready to eat.

MORE SMASHED NEW POTATOES . . . AND LEFTOVERS

Tartiflette. Make a tartiflette-style homity pie by omitting the leek and adding 3½ oz [100 g] fried bacon lardoons to the potato mixture, then laying 7 oz [200 g] reblochon cheese on top. Serves 4 as a big lunch.

Portuguese "punched" potatoes. Prepare 1 quantity Smashed new potatoes with butter and mint, then roast in the oven at 350°F [180°C] 35 minutes, until brown and crunchy. So good! Serves 4 as a side dish.

Smashed with capers, egg, and sorrel. If you have leftover Smashed new potatoes with butter and mint, dress them with capers, extra virgin oil, chopped sorrel—or other soft herbs such as tarragon or basil—and chopped hard-boiled egg.

Homity pie

This really is humble pie: leeks, potatoes, and cheese. I was brought up eating Cranks's delicious wholemeal recipe, and this is a variation. In order to stay true to its make-do-and-mend roots, I've suggested you use up all your odds and ends of cheese from the refrigerator. Homity pie tastes best cold, so it makes great buffet or picnic food. Serves 4 as a generous lunch.

For the filling
1 quantity Smashed new potatoes with butter and mint
1 large onion, sliced
1 leek, finely sliced
2 garlic cloves, roughly chopped
Leaves from 1 sprig thyme
Glug of light olive oil
⅝ cup [150 ml] heavy cream
4 sprigs parsley, roughly chopped
7 oz [200 g] mixed cheese (use up odds and ends)

For the shortcrust pastry case
1⅔ cups [200 g] all-purpose flour, preferably spelt, plus more to dust
7 Tbsp [100 g] cold butter, cut into small cubes
1 egg, lightly beaten

To make the pastry case, put the flour, butter, and a pinch of salt into a blender and blend until the butter is combined into the flour, then add 4 Tbsp cold water. Pulse-blend 3 times, adding another spoon of water if it is not forming into a ball, then bring the dough together with your hands. Wrap in a clean plastic bag and chill 30 minutes in the refrigerator.

Preheat the oven to 375°F [190°C]. Roll out the pastry on a lightly floured surface to about ⅛ in [4 mm] thickness. Use the pastry to line an 8 in [20 cm] case, making sure it is pushed down into all the corners and that it overhangs at the top (this will stop the pastry shrinking back). Prick all over with a fork to help stop the pastry puffing up. Put in the oven 20 minutes until just cooked. This is called blind baking. Trim the excess pastry from the edges with a knife, brush with the egg, filling any holes or cracks, then return to the oven 3 minutes. Let cool.

Meanwhile, sauté the onion, leek, and garlic with the thyme slowly in the light olive oil 20 minutes until soft and caramelized. Mix in the potatoes, cream, and parsley. Taste and season generously.

Fill the pastry case with the potato mixture. Grate hard cheese and cut soft cheese into small pieces, then arrange on top. The pie should be almost overflowing.

Bake in the hot oven 10 to 15 minutes, until the cheese has melted and is bubbling with some charred spots. Let cool a little before serving.

STORAGE The smashed potatoes and the pie keep well in sealed containers in the refrigerator 4 or 5 days. I like them both best eaten cold.

Eating
BROCCOLI

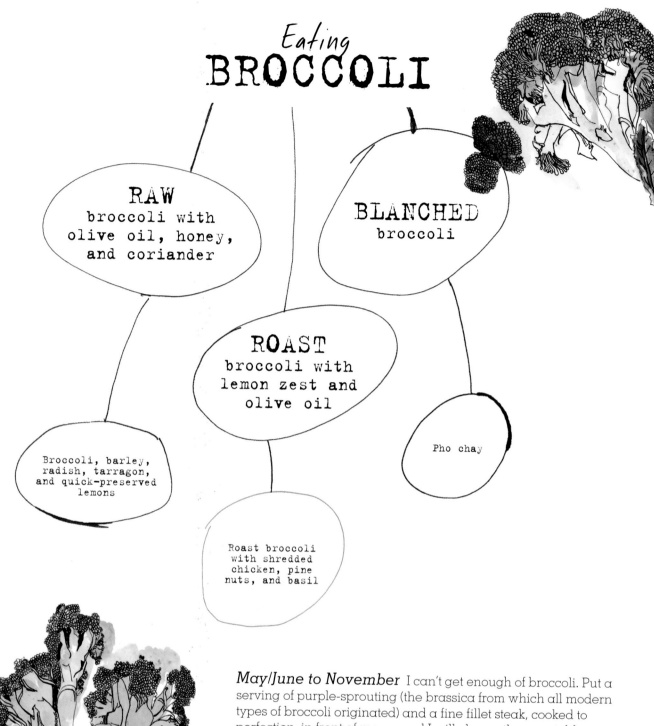

RAW
broccoli with
olive oil, honey,
and coriander

BLANCHED
broccoli

ROAST
broccoli with
lemon zest and
olive oil

Broccoli, barley,
radish, tarragon,
and quick-preserved
lemons

Pho chay

Roast broccoli
with shredded
chicken, pine
nuts, and basil

May/June to November I can't get enough of broccoli. Put a serving of purple-sprouting (the brassica from which all modern types of broccoli originated) and a fine fillet steak, cooked to perfection, in front of me . . . and I will choose the vegetable every time. Roast it, eat it raw, or blanch it in bubbling hot water. Serve dressed with good olive oil and some salt and dine like a king. That's not to say I don't love our domesticated green variety of broccoli just as much; you get a lot more veg for your money and it's almost as nutritious. Treat it the same; cook it fast. Broccoli is of course very good for us—really high in vitamin C—and it also contains immune-boosting nutrients.

Buy broccoli heads or stems that are firm and green and not wrapped in cellophane so you can gauge their freshness. Keep them in a clean plastic bag in the refrigerator, as the broccoli will keep for longer. If the top yellows slightly, don't worry, it's still fine to eat. People often waste the stalk, but don't make the same mistake! I like to peel it and eat the core as a treat while cooking, but have added it to my dishes here and suggest you do the same.

Raw broccoli with olive oil, honey, and coriander

The more raw food we can eat the better. Raw broccoli is full of nutrients and enzymes and this salad is a quick and easy way to make a simple vegetable taste great. Serves 4 as a side salad.

10½ oz [300 g] broccoli, extra virgin olive oil, juice of ¼ lemon, 1 tsp raw local honey, 1 tsp coriander seeds

Cut the broccoli into bite-size florets. Peel the outer skin from the stalk and chop the soft core into cubes. Put in a bowl with the florets and season with extra virgin oil, the lemon juice, and honey. Toast the coriander seeds in a dry pan until aromatic, then crush them slightly in a mortar and pestle and sprinkle over the top.

MORE RAW BROCCOLI . . . AND LEFTOVERS
Salad with rice, nori, and ginger. Cook ¼ cup [50 g] brown rice, rinse to cool it down, and allow to dry thoroughly in a colander. Add it to ½ quantity Raw broccoli with olive oil, honey, and coriander. Make a dressing by finely chopping a small thumb of ginger root and mixing it with 2 Tbsp soy sauce and a sprinkling of sesame seeds. Toss with the broccoli and rice and top with nori seaweed, torn into flakes. Serves 2 as a light lunch.

Tempura. Make a batter by whisking ¾ cup [100 g] spelt flour with ½ tsp baking powder. Pour in ⅝ cup [150 ml] cold sparkling water. Heat a small saucepan of flavorless vegetable oil no more than one-third full. Check it's hot by dropping in a blob of batter: if it bubbles and rises straight to the top, it's at the right temperature. Reduce the heat to medium. Using tongs or chopsticks, dip the florets from 1 quantity Raw broccoli with olive oil, honey, and cilantro into the batter, shake, then place them in the hot oil, cooking only a few at a time so the temperature of the oil doesn't drop. Fry 2 or 3 minutes, until the florets are floating and light brown in color. Remove from the oil and drain on paper towels. Serve with sweet chili sauce. Serves 2 as a light lunch or appetizer.

Broccoli, barley, radish, tarragon, and quick-preserved lemons

This is a filling salad, great to eat as the weather warms up. It will keep very well in the refrigerator, so make sure you save any extra for lunch the next day. Serves 4 as an accompaniment.

1 quantity Raw broccoli with olive oil, honey, and coriander
¼ cup [50 g] pearl barley
4 radishes, finely sliced
6 scallions, finely sliced
Small bunch tarragon and chives, or any other soft herbs you have, chopped
¼ Quick-preserved lemon (see page 63), flesh removed, skin chopped into slivers
2 tsp cumin seeds
1 tsp sweet paprika
3½ Tbsp [50 ml] light olive oil
3 garlic cloves, finely sliced
2 tsp sesame seeds
1 Tbsp raw local honey

Boil the barley in plenty of water 20 to 30 minutes, until soft. Be careful not to overcook it, as it keeps swelling and becomes fluffy; I like it best a little chewy. Mix the barley with the broccoli, radishes, scallions, herbs, and preserved lemon.

In a small skillet, cook the cumin seeds, paprika, olive oil, garlic, and sesame seeds together gently for one minute to release all the flavors. Mix into the salad thoroughly with the honey, coating all the barley.

STORAGE The raw broccoli is best eaten immediately. The salad keeps well in a sealed container in the refrigerator 4 days. Return it to room temperature before serving.

Roast broccoli with lemon zest and olive oil

This is a winning dish: surprisingly tasty and full of robust and savory flavors. If your broccoli is looking a bit tired, then roasting is a good way to use it up, as the flavors are intensified and sweetened. Serves 4 to 5 as a side dish.

14 oz [400 g] broccoli, light olive oil, finely grated unwaxed lemon zest

Preheat the oven to 350°F [180°C]. Cut the broccoli into large florets, then peel the stalk and cut it into chunks. Toss them in light olive oil and salt and pepper, then grate a little of the lemon zest over the top. Roast in the oven 20 to 30 minutes, until charred in places and cooked right through.

MORE ROAST BROCCOLI . . . AND LEFTOVERS
With chili, ginger and cashews. Cook ½ quantity Roast broccoli with lemon zest and olive oil, adding ½ finely chopped jalapeño chili, a small thumb of ginger root, chopped, and 2 Tbsp cashews. Serves 4 to 5 as a side dish, or 2 for lunch with brown rice.

In a blue cheese gratin. Preheat the oven to 350°F [180°C]. Put 1 quantity Roast broccoli with lemon zest and olive oil in a small, deep ovenproof dish. Crumble 5¼ oz [150 g] blue cheese over the top and return to the oven 10 minutes to melt the cheese. Serves 5 as a rich side dish.

Roast broccoli with shredded chicken, pine nuts, and basil

A really satisfying lunch or easy dinner. Chicken thighs are relatively cheap when compared to breasts, so spend the savings on free-range or organic meat, whatever you can afford. Serves 2 as a light meal.

1 quantity Roast broccoli with lemon zest and olive oil, assembled but not yet cooked
2 chicken thighs
Light olive oil
Sprig rosemary
5 tsp pine nuts
A grating of unwaxed lemon zest
12 basil leaves
⅔ cup [50 g] parmesan

Preheat the oven to 375°F [190°C]. Put the chicken thighs on a baking sheet, season with salt and pepper, drizzle with the oil, and tuck the rosemary underneath. Roast 15 minutes.

Reduce the oven temperature to 350°F [180°C] and put the broccoli in to roast 20 to 30 minutes, as described left.

After the chicken has been in the oven 35 minutes, check it is cooked by inserting a knife to the bone and wiggling it. If the juices are clear it is cooked, though the bone itself may still be a little red and that's fine. If the juices run at all pink, cook a few more minutes before checking again. Remove from the oven and rest 5 minutes.

Place the pine nuts in a small dry skillet over medium heat. Toast 3 to 5 minutes; you want them to be golden brown with dark patches. Pour into a small bowl. Shred the chicken from the bone and toss on to the baking sheet with the warm broccoli. Serve on a platter scattered with the pine nuts and the lemon zest. Tear the basil leaves over and add shards of parmesan, shaved with a vegetable peeler.

STORAGE Roast broccoli will keep in a sealed container in the refrigerator 3 days. Blast it in a single layer in a very hot oven to reheat. The salad will keep in a sealed container in the refrigerator 4 days; return to room temperature before serving.

Blanched broccoli

So simple, rejuvenating, and nutritious. Broccoli takes only minutes to prepare and blanch, so cook it last when the rest of the meal is ready; don't let it hang around. Serves 3 to 4.

10½ oz [300 g] broccoli, extra virgin olive oil, soy sauce (optional)

Rinse the broccoli and cut it into large florets. Peel the stalk and cut the core into cubes. Bring a large pan of water to a boil and salt it generously. When the water is at a rolling boil, drop in the broccoli. Get a colander ready in the sink. After 4 minutes, check to see if the broccoli is cooked by pushing a knife into it. If it gives but still has a firmness, it is ready. Drain immediately, leave to steam in the colander 1 minute, then return to the pan. Drizzle with extra virgin oil and some soy sauce, if using.

MORE BLANCHED BROCCOLI . . . AND LEFTOVERS
Pho ca. For a change from Pho chay, divide 3½ oz [100 g] chopped fish—such as sea bass, salmon, or trout—among the bowls of noodles, then ladle the hot stock over the top. The fish will cook through perfectly. Serves 4 to 6.

Creamed broccoli soup with goat's cheese. Blend 7 oz [200 g] Blanched broccoli with 1 cup [250 ml] of its cooking liquid and 1¾ oz [50 g] goat's cheese until smooth. Serve hot with more crumbled goat's cheese on top. Serves 2.

Pho chay

I call this my mega-amazing-rejuvenating-super-soup and eat it whenever I'm feeling in need of a detox. The chilies and fresh vegetables replenish and refresh. Serves 4 to 6.

1 quantity Blanched broccoli, trimmings
 added to the stock (see below)
5¼ oz [150 g] brown or white rice noodles, broken
 into pieces
2 scallions, finely chopped, trimmings put in the stock
3½ oz [100 g] bean sprouts or home-grown sprouts (see
 page 126)
1 chili, sliced on the diagonal, trimmings put in the stock,
 plus more chopped chilies to serve
Small bunch cilantro, mint, and basil, stalks put in
 the stock
1 lemongrass stalk, finely sliced, outer layer put in
 the stock
2 garlic cloves, finely sliced
4¼ oz [120 g] shiitake or chestnut mushrooms, finely sliced,
 stalks put in the stock
1 carrot, thinly sliced, trimmings put in the stock
Tamari or soy sauce
1 lime, quartered, to serve

For the quick Asian stock
1 garlic clove, grated
Small thumb ginger root with skin, grated
1 small onion, grated
1 carrot, grated
2 cloves
Small piece cinnamon stick
2 star anise

Make the stock: pour 4½ cups [1 L] water into a large saucepan and add the ingredients, with all the vegetable trimmings. Bring to a boil, cover, and simmer 30 minutes. Place a sieve over a saucepan and pass the liquid through it, then return to the pan and to low heat.

Cook the noodles according to the packet instructions, then split them between 4 or 6 warmed bowls. Decorate each with some scallions, bean sprouts, chili, and herbs. Return the stock to a rolling boil. Add the lemongrass, garlic, mushrooms, carrot, and broccoli. Boil 3 minutes, then ladle into the bowls. Offer the extra chili, herbs, and tamari or soy sauce and lime quarters, for guests to season their broth as they prefer.

STORAGE Blanched broccoli will keep 3 days in a sealed container in the refrigerator. Blanch briefly once more to reheat. Pho chay is best eaten ultra-fresh, but will keep 4 days in a sealed container in the refrigerator. Reheat to just under boiling point to serve.

COOK NATURAL Bean sprouts come in wastefully large packets and you'll often find you run out of things to do with them before they go off, so sprout your own; there are guides on YouTube. If you bought a big pack, add them to all your salads and stir-fries.

Raw scallions with chili and lime

A simple, fresh way to prepare scallions with minimal effort. This is great with a curry. Serves 1 as a side salad.

3 scallions, dash of extra virgin olive oil, ½ chili, juice of ½ lime

Wash the scallions and trim the roots and the very tops if they're dry. Slice finely. Dress with the extra virgin oil. Finely chop the chili and scatter over the top with the lime juice.

Trout ceviche with crispy skin and tortilla chips

Ceviche is Peru's national dish. Peruvian fishmongers make it in big jars at the end of the day as a way of preserving their fish and giving it new life. It tastes so fresh, punchy, and full of flavor. Rainbow trout is widely farmed and is available at most fishmongers all year round. It is a good choice of fish, as the farming methods have a relatively low impact on local eco-systems. Serves 6 as an appetizer.

1 quantity Raw scallions with chili and lime
7 oz [200 g] trout fillets
3 sprigs of cilantro, stalks finely chopped, leaves roughly chopped
Finely grated zest of 1 lime, plus the juice of 2
2 fresh or stale tortillas, cut into triangles or strips
Flavorless vegetable oil

Remove the trout skin and set aside. (Ask your fishmonger to do this if you prefer.)

Chop the trout into ⅜ in [1 cm] pieces, discarding any pin-bones you see, and put the fish in a bowl. Stir in the scallions, cilantro, and lime zest and juice. Leave 20 minutes to allow the lime juice to "cook" the fish; you will see it turn opaque.

To make the crispy skin and tortilla chips, shallow-fry them both in vegetable oil in a hot skillet or wok 1 minute on either side, until they have color. Remove from the skillet, then let cool and drain on paper towels.

Serve the ceviche in a bowl or glasses with the crispy skin and tortilla chips sticking out at jaunty angles.

STORAGE The raw scallions are best eaten immediately. Keep the ceviche in a sealed sterilized jar (see page 52) up to 4 days in the refrigerator. Return to room temperature to serve.

MORE RAW SCALLIONS . . . AND LEFTOVERS
Bean salad. Mix 1 quantity Raw scallions with chili and lime with 14 oz [400 g] can of drained, rinsed mixed beans, for a more substantial dish. Serves 3 to 4 as a side salad.

Fish pie. To make a zesty pie, preheat the oven to 350°F [180°C]. Mix 1 quantity Trout ceviche (without crispy skin or tortilla chips) with 7 Tbsp [100 ml] crème fraîche and put into an ovenproof dish. Top with mashed potato and bake in the hot oven 30 minutes, until hot right through. Serves 2 to 3.

Steamed scallions with ginger

Whole scallions steam particularly well and eat like any greens, with an added savory onion kick. Serves 2 as a side dish.

1 bunch of scallions, 1 garlic clove, a few slices of ginger root, glug of light olive oil

Wash the scallions and trim the roots and the very tops if they're dry. Cut each in half, crosswise. Heat a heavy-based sauté pan with a lid over medium heat, then add the scallions with a splash of water. Slice the garlic and add to the pan with the ginger and oil. Cover and steam 5 minutes. Remove the lid and fry 1 minute to allow any juices to evaporate. These taste great with grilled meat, or with Chinese-style steamed fish.

MORE STEAMED SCALLIONS . . . AND LEFTOVERS
Frittata. Make 1 quantity Steamed scallions with ginger. Beat 3 eggs with salt and pepper and add to the scallion pan. Fry gently until the egg is just cooked, adding herbs if you like. Serves 2.

Summer rolls. The cooked tilapia makes a great summer roll filling. Dip rice paper wrappers in water until supple, roll leftover fish up in them along with any sprigs of soft herbs you have, then serve with Thai chili dipping sauce.

Banh mi of tilapia and scallions

Banh mi is a Vietnamese-style baguette, an utterly delicious fusion of cultures. The steamed scallions really shine in this dish and work well with the fish and turmeric. Tilapia is a safe choice when considering fish stocks, as they are a well-managed breed that is not overfished. If you'd rather use a fish caught closer to home, choose sustainably sourced cod. Serves 4 for lunch or 12 as a canapé.

1 quantity Steamed scallions with ginger
½ tsp turmeric
1 Tbsp spelt or all-purpose flour
15¾ oz [450 g] tilapia, cut into cubes
Glug of flavorless vegetable oil
2 garlic cloves, finely chopped
1 baguette
Small bunch dill, thick stalks finely chopped, fronds roughly chopped
1 turnip, peeled and grated
Juice of 1 lime

Mix the turmeric and flour with salt and pepper and put the mixture in a shallow dish. Toss the tilapia in the seasoned flour.

Place a skillet over medium heat with the vegetable oil. Fry the fish 2 or 3 minutes until it browns, then turn and color the other side. Add the garlic and fry 1 minute more. Check the fish is cooked by cutting a piece in half: it should be opaque at the center. Remove from the heat.

Cut open the baguette—leaving a hinge—but don't prize it open, as you want the baguette to hold shut later. Stuff it with the fish, dill, turnip, and scallions. Squeeze over the lime juice and serve.

STORAGE Both the steamed scallions and the cooked fish will keep in sealed containers in the refrigerator 3 days, but are best fresh. Return both to room temperature to serve.

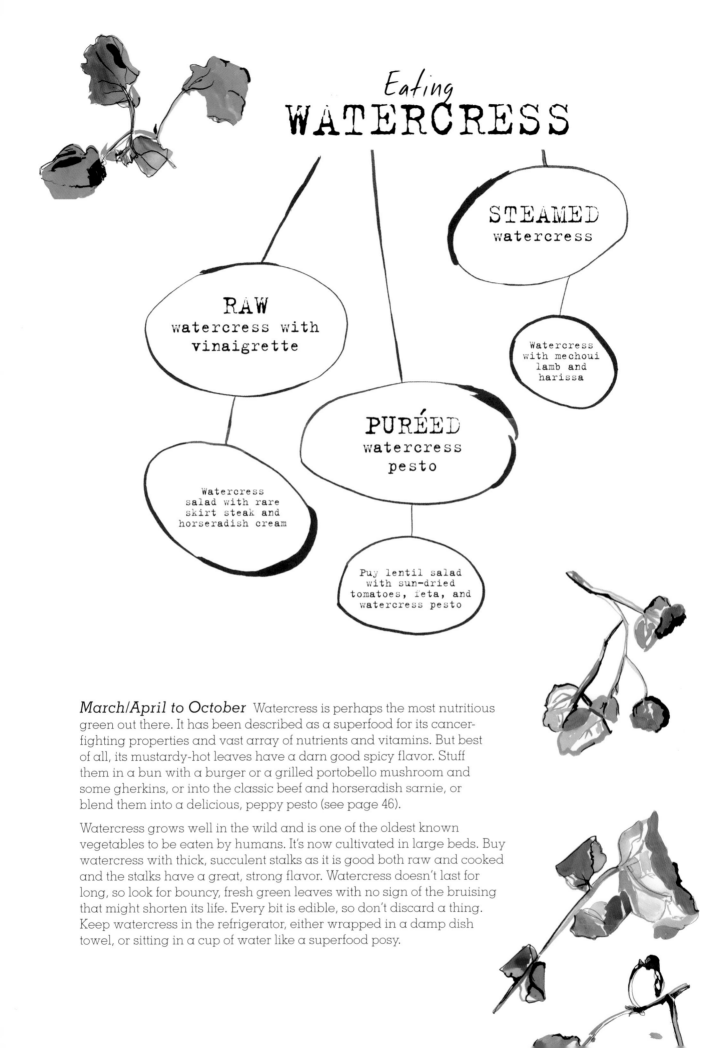

Eating
WATERCRESS

STEAMED
watercress

Watercress
with mechoui
lamb and
harissa

RAW
watercress with
vinaigrette

PURÉED
watercress
pesto

Watercress
salad with rare
skirt steak and
horseradish cream

Puy lentil salad
with sun-dried
tomatoes, feta, and
watercress pesto

March/April to October Watercress is perhaps the most nutritious green out there. It has been described as a superfood for its cancer-fighting properties and vast array of nutrients and vitamins. But best of all, its mustardy-hot leaves have a darn good spicy flavor. Stuff them in a bun with a burger or a grilled portobello mushroom and some gherkins, or into the classic beef and horseradish sarnie, or blend them into a delicious, peppy pesto (see page 46).

Watercress grows well in the wild and is one of the oldest known vegetables to be eaten by humans. It's now cultivated in large beds. Buy watercress with thick, succulent stalks as it is good both raw and cooked and the stalks have a great, strong flavor. Watercress doesn't last for long, so look for bouncy, fresh green leaves with no sign of the bruising that might shorten its life. Every bit is edible, so don't discard a thing. Keep watercress in the refrigerator, either wrapped in a damp dish towel, or sitting in a cup of water like a superfood posy.

Raw watercress with vinaigrette

Watercress is brimming with vital minerals. This is a simplistic salad dressed with a vinaigrette that can be kept in a jar in the refrigerator for whenever you need it. Serves 2 as a side dish.

7 Tbsp [100 ml] red wine or sherry vinegar, 1¼ cups [300 ml] extra virgin olive oil, 2 Tbsp whole grain mustard, 3 oz [80 g] watercress

To make the dressing, find a 2⅛ cups [500 ml] jar. Pour in the vinegar and extra virgin oil. Add the mustard and season with salt and pepper. Put the lid on and keep it in the refrigerator. Whenever you need some vinaigrette, give the jar a good shake to emulsify the oil and vinegar. Wash the watercress and shake it dry. Toss with 1 to 2 Tbsp of the dressing just before serving, to keep the leaves perky and fresh.

MORE RAW WATERCRESS . . . AND LEFTOVERS
Tempura. If you have leftover undressed watercress leaves, eat them up quickly as irresistible tempura. Make a tempura batter and deep-fry big pinches of watercress—coated in the batter—in flavorless vegetable oil (see page 31). Serve with sweet chili dipping sauce.

Watercress, persimmon, and ricotta with chili. Persimmons are in season during early spring and are delicious in savory dishes as well as sweet. Slice them thinly and arrange on a plate with Raw watercress with vinaigrette. Drizzle with extra virgin oil, sprinkle with chili flakes, and dot chunks of ricotta around and about.

Watercress salad with rare skirt steak and horseradish cream

Watercress, beef, and horseradish is a classic combination. Homemade horseradish cream steps it up a notch and makes a really special yet simple lunch. If you don't eat meat, you could try this salad with Roast broccoli instead (see page 33). Serves 4.

For the steak and salad
1 quantity Raw watercress with vinaigrette, not yet dressed with the vinaigrette
1⅛ lb [500 g] skirt steak (bavette)
Light olive oil

For the horseradish sauce
14 Tbsp [200 ml] crème fraîche
1 Tbsp red wine vinegar
Thumb of horseradish, grated, or to taste

Start with the sauce. Mix the crème fraîche with the vinegar and season with salt and pepper. Grate in the horseradish and taste, adding more if you like. Be careful, though, as the root is pretty hot stuff.

Season the steak with salt and pepper and rub with a little oil. Heat a griddle pan over high heat. Sear the steak 2 minutes each side for rare, or 4 minutes each side for medium. Set aside to rest 5 to 10 minutes.

Dress the watercress with its vinaigrette and arrange the leaves on 4 plates. Slice the steak thinly and lay it over the watercress. Spoon over some horseradish cream to serve.

STORAGE Watercress doesn't keep very well, so it needs to be eaten quickly. Store the undressed leaves in a damp dish towel or a cup of water in the refrigerator 1 or 2 days. The cooked steak will keep well stored in the same way 3 or 4 days, but return it to room temperature before serving.

Steamed watercress

Watercress is a versatile green that is good when cooked, and it's quick and easy to wilt or steam it in a pan. Stir it into couscous with roasted vegetables, serve as a side vegetable, or make it into soup (see below). Choose good, strong watercress with robust, thick stalks. Serves 4 as a side dish.

1⅓ lb [600 g] watercress, 1 garlic clove, glug light olive oil

Wash the watercress and chop roughly. Slice the garlic. Place a skillet that has a lid over medium-high heat with the oil. When it starts to sizzle, drop in the garlic and watercress, the latter still a little wet from washing. Put the lid on 1 minute, then uncover and stir. As soon as the watercress has wilted, it is ready.

MORE STEAMED WATERCRESS . . . AND LEFTOVERS
Watercress soup. Boil 3½ oz [100 g] potatoes in 3⅓ cups [800 ml] vegetable stock until soft. Add ½ quantity Steamed watercress, then blend immediately to get the brightest green soup. Add a dash of cream. Serves 4.

Lamb ragu. To make a delicious pasta sauce, fry 1 finely chopped onion in light olive oil until soft. Add 7 oz [200 g] leftover Mechoui lamb and a 14 oz [400 g] can of chopped tomatoes. Simmer 15 minutes, then adjust the seasoning and toss over cooked, drained spelt or wholewheat pasta. Serves 2.

Watercress with mechoui lamb and harissa

Mechoui lamb is slow-cooked, then rested for as long as possible so it steams in its own juices and becomes succulent and aromatic. Watercress works well with this dish, making a delicious iron-rich accompaniment. Serves 6.

1 quantity Steamed watercress
2 tsp coriander seeds
2 tsp cumin seeds
2 Tbsp butter
1 tsp sweet paprika
Finely grated zest of ½ unwaxed lemon
3 garlic cloves, finely chopped
2¼ lb [1 kg] lamb shoulder (the knuckle is the most succulent)
Harissa sauce, to serve

Preheat the oven to 400°F [200°C]. Grind the coriander and cumin in a mortar and pestle. Mash the butter with the spices, lemon zest, and garlic, adding 1 tsp each of salt and freshly ground black pepper.

Rub the flavored butter all over the lamb, making sure it goes into any nooks and crannies, then place in a roasting tin (if you have one with a lid, use that). Roast 15 to 20 minutes until brown, then remove from the oven, baste with the buttery juices and cover tightly with the lid, or with foil. Reduce the oven temperature to 300°F [150°C] and return the lamb. Cook slowly at least 3 hours, checking the meat halfway through to make sure the roasting tin isn't drying out. Spoon some of the buttery juices over the top as you do so.

Remove from the oven, baste again, then rest, covered with the lid or the foil, 30 minutes. Skim the excess fat from the top of the juices. Pull the meat off the bones and mix it with the cooking juices. Serve mixed with the watercress, offering harissa sauce on the side.

STORAGE Both the watercress and the shredded lamb and juices will keep well 4 days in sealed containers in the refrigerator. Reheat both in a pan until hot right through and adjust the seasoning if necessary.

COOK NATURAL Find a butcher—or search for farms online—that sell lamb that has been reared locally and 100 percent grass fed. This is their natural diet, so it is better for the animal and for the environment than food supplements that could contain any number of chemicals and may have been imported from across the world. Lamb shoulder is a delicious and relatively cheap cut; look for lamb that has a good amount of fat and is relatively dark in color. It can be cooked pink, but takes well to a long, slow roast.

Puréed watercress pesto

A great backup dish to have in the refrigerator, ready for those moments when there's no time to cook. It's easy to make and works out relatively cheap when compared to the traditional basil version. Makes 1 small jar.

3½ oz [100 g] watercress, 2 Tbsp pine nuts, small thumb of horseradish, grated (optional), ⅜ cup [30 g] finely grated parmesan, 3½ Tbsp [50 ml] olive oil, juice of ½ lemon, or to taste

Rinse the watercress and shake dry. Toast the pine nuts in a dry pan 3 to 5 minutes; they should be golden brown with dark patches. Tip into a blender with all the other ingredients, using just half the lemon juice. Season with salt and pepper and pulse-blend to a rough paste. Taste and adjust the salt, pepper, and lemon juice.

MORE PURÉED WATERCRESS PESTO . . .
AND LEFTOVERS
Pesto potatoes. Add a spoon of Puréed watercress pesto to boiled new potatoes and mix well. Dress with more finely grated parmesan, if you like.

Super-tasty veggie burgers. If you have any leftover salad, pulse blend it with a spoon of spelt flour a few times so that it becomes mushy but still has texture. Form the mixture into burgers, then fry slowly in light olive oil 5 minutes on each side until a little crispy and hot right through. Serve wrapped in lettuce leaves instead of rolls, with chili sauce if you wish.

Puy lentil salad with sun-dried tomatoes, feta, and watercress pesto

A lovely, simple salad that keeps very well in the refrigerator, this makes a great lunch or buffet dish. Play around and add different grilled vegetables, whichever are your favorites or that need using up. Serves 6 as a salad entree.

1 quantity Puréed watercress pesto
3½ oz [100 g] Puy lentils
5¼ oz [150 g] (about) zucchini, a mixture of yellow and
   green if possible, sliced lengthwise ⅜ in [1 cm] thick
3 scallions
Light olive oil
1¾ oz [50 g] sun-dried tomatoes, or oven-dried tomatoes
   (see page 14), chopped
2 tsp flat-leaf parsley, stalks finely chopped, leaves
   roughly chopped
¼ red onion, finely chopped
3½ oz [100 g] feta cheese, crumbled

Boil the lentils in plenty of water 15 to 20 minutes. Remove from the heat when tender, with a little bite. Drain in a colander and cool under running water. Leave to dry in the colander.

Toss the zucchini and scallions in a little light olive oil and season with salt. Heat a griddle pan over high heat and slightly char the zucchini and onions on both sides. Let cool, then cut the zucchinis into 2 in [5 cm] long pieces and finely chop the onions.

Place all the ingredients in a bowl and turn, evenly coating everything in the pesto.

STORAGE The watercress pesto will keep in a jar in the refrigerator 1 week; the salad 3 days in a sealed container in the refrigerator. Return the salad to room temperature before serving.

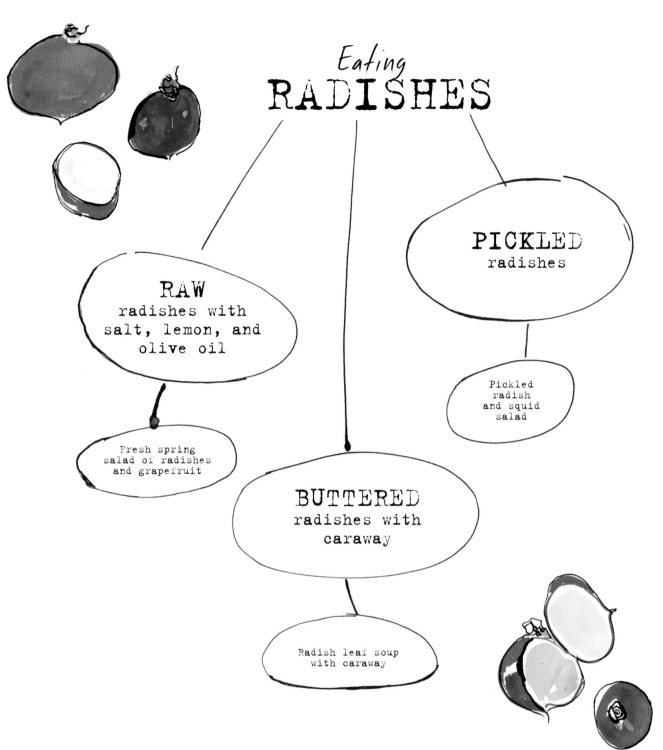

Eating RADISHES

RAW
radishes with
salt, lemon, and
olive oil

Fresh spring
salad of radishes
and grapefruit

PICKLED
radishes

Pickled
radish
and squid
salad

BUTTERED
radishes with
caraway

Radish leaf soup
with caraway

April to September Radishes grow fast: just 3 weeks in the soil produces a root big enough to warrant the chop. I love the spicy, peppery varieties that burn your mouth like a hot mustard leaf. But there are many: long French breakfast and—these days becoming easier to find—bulbous purple, red, and white globes. Grow them in pots about your house or on your windowsill. Snack on them like chips, fresh from the soil. It's all about the crunch. Just don't waste the leaves. They are nutritious and add a peppery twist to salads, or can replace spinach or watercress in soups and stews (see page 50). The root can be eaten raw with local honey and vinegar, on toast with butter and salt, or it can be pickled and served with fish.

The leaves deteriorate quickly, so are a good indication of how fresh your radish is in the store or at the market. Look for crisp leaves and a firm root. Store them in the refrigerator, removing the leaves and keeping them chilled separately in a tub or clean plastic bag. Soak the roots in ice-cold water before serving, to make sure they are ultra-crisp.

Raw radishes with salt, lemon, and olive oil

For this dish, you want the freshest, crunchiest radishes. If they have squeaky-fresh tops, too, save them in the refrigerator to cook as greens, or add to Radish leaf soup with caraway (see page 50). Serves 2 to 3 as a side dish.

5¼ oz [150 g] radishes (keep the leaves if they are fresh), juice of ¼ lemon, extra virgin olive oil

Wash the radishes well and cut them into quarters from top to tail. Dress with the lemon juice, some extra virgin oil, and a sprinkle of salt. Eat straightaway.

MORE RAW RADISHES . . . AND LEFTOVERS
With crab. Make the salad as above right, then mix in 3½ oz [100 g] white crab meat. Serves 4.

Radish and cucumber raita. This is a simple variation on a classic. I like it best made with peppery radishes. Mix equal amounts of finely sliced radishes, cucumber, and live yogurt together with some roughly chopped cilantro or parsley. Season with salt, pepper, and freshly ground cumin to taste. Add a squeeze of lemon juice and a drizzle of olive oil and serve with curry or a Paratha (see page 164).

Fresh spring salad of radishes and grapefruit

A simple, colorful, and very pretty salad that makes the most of spring vegetables. Serves 4.

1 quantity Raw radishes with salt, lemon, and olive oil
1 grapefruit, white, pink, or red, whichever you prefer
½ red onion, finely chopped
½ radicchio (use the other half in Grilled salad of zucchini, radicchio, basil, and mozzarella, see page 73), shredded
1 Little Gem lettuce, leaves separated and washed
About 10 chives, cut into 2 in [5 cm] lengths
2 Tbsp extra virgin olive oil
Juice of ½ lemon

Peel the grapefruit with a knife, removing the pith and skin. Cut it into slices, flicking out seeds as you see them, then cut the slices into quarters. Soak the chopped onion in a small bowl of cold water 5 minutes, to make it both milder in flavor and crisper in texture. Drain.

Combine all the fruit, vegetables, leaves, and herbs, then dress with the extra virgin oil, lemon juice, and salt and pepper. Serve immediately.

STORAGE The raw radishes are best eaten immediately. Prepare all the elements of the salad ahead of time if you wish and keep them, separately, in sealed containers in the refrigerator. Once dressed, the salad won't keep for long, so dress it just before you take it to the table.

Buttered radishes
with caraway

This is a good recipe if your radishes are a little old. But, if they're fresher and have sprightly tops, cut them off, shred both the stalks and leaves, and set aside to use in the recipe. Serves 1 to 2 as a side dish.

3½ oz [100 g] radishes and leaves (optional), knob of butter, pinch of caraway seeds, flat-leaf parsley

Wash the radishes, then cut them into halves, or quarters if they are really big. Put the butter in a heavy-based skillet and place over medium heat. Add the radishes and cook slowly 3 minutes, until their color dulls slightly and bleeds into the flesh. Be careful that the pan doesn't get too hot, otherwise the butter will burn. Add the radish leaves (if you have them), the caraway, and a sprinkle of salt and pepper and cook a further 30 seconds to allow the aromas to come to life. Chop the parsley and toss into the pan to serve.

Radish leaf soup
with caraway

This dish is shockingly good; it's a great thrifty use of the leaves and simple to make (you can try it with watercress instead of radish leaves too, if you like). I like to thicken it with rice, as it gives a velvety texture. Serves 4.

1 quantity Buttered radishes with caraway, plus 4 radishes, grated, to serve
1 onion, finely sliced
1 small zucchini, roughly chopped
Green top of 1 leek, roughly sliced
6 mint leaves, stalk(s) reserved
1 bay leaf
1 celery stick, roughly sliced
3 garlic cloves, roughly chopped
Good glug of light olive oil
¼ cup [50 g] risotto rice or short-grain brown rice (from health food stores)
5¼ oz [150 g] radish leaves
Knob of butter

Sauté the onion, zucchini, leek, mint stalks, bay leaf, celery, and garlic in the light olive oil 10 minutes over low heat. Add 2⅞ cups [700 ml] water, the radishes, and the rice. Bring to a boil, then reduce the heat and simmer 25 minutes, or until the rice is soft.

Remove the mint stalks, add the radish and mint leaves, then blend until smooth and a vibrant green. Serve as soon as possible to keep the color, and be careful not to reboil the soup, or it will fade. Serve each bowl topped with grated radish and a knob of butter.

STORAGE The soup will lose some of its green vibrancy, but will keep fine 3 days in a sealed container in the refrigerator. Reheat to just below boiling point to serve. The buttered radishes with caraway are best eaten immediately.

MORE BUTTERED RADISHES . . . AND LEFTOVERS
With rare beef. Cook a steak with 1 quantity Buttered radishes and caraway 3 minutes, then slice thinly and serve with the browned butter. Serves 2.

Radish and anchovy butter. If you have any spare uncooked radishes in the bunch, grate them and combine with softened butter and 1 pounded anchovy, or to taste. Add salt and a sprinkle of caraway and serve on toasts.

Pickled radishes

Delicious to eat as soon as they're pickled, these are great on their own: intensely salty, sweet, and sour. Makes one 1⅛ lb [500 g] jar.

1 bunch radishes, 1 carrot, ⅔ cup [160 ml] rice vinegar, 1 sprig thyme, 1 tsp coriander seeds, 2 garlic cloves, 2 Tbsp rapadura or raw cane sugar, 1½ Tbsp sea salt

Clean the radishes and remove the leaves. (Keep them for Radish leaf soup with caraway, see page 50.) Finely slice the carrot. In a small saucepan, combine the vinegar, thyme, coriander, garlic, sugar, and sea salt with 9 Tbsp [140 ml] water. Bring to a boil, stirring, add the carrot and radishes, then remove from the heat. Sterilize a glass jar (see below right), fill with the hot radishes while the jar is warm, then seal.

MORE PICKLED RADISHES . . . AND LEFTOVERS
Fried pickles with sour cream. When you make Pickled radishes, add some seeded large batons of cucumber. When ready to fry, prepare a deep-fryer, or fill a large saucepan no more than one-third full with vegetable oil. While the oil is heating, make a batter: mix 7 Tbsp [100 ml] water with ⅞ cup [100 g] spelt or all-purpose flour and 2 Tbsp flavorless vegetable oil. Take some mixed pickles, dust with a little more flour, then dip in the batter one by one. Deep-fry just a few at a time, so the temperature of the oil does not drop, turning until golden brown (see page 31 for further deep-frying instructions). Serve with sour cream.

Banh mi. Pickles are delicious in Banh mi (see page 40). Add these pickles to the filling.

Pickled radish and squid salad

Pickling is so easy and a brilliant way to preserve any leftover vegetables, or even fish! Squid is so tender when pickled like this, plus it's fun to cook. Serves 4 as an appetizer.

For the salad
1 quantity Pickled radishes
10½ oz [300 g] squid, prepared weight
¼ cucumber, cut into batons or sticks
Few sprigs cilantro, stalks finely chopped, leaves roughly chopped

For the dressing
1 Tbsp fish sauce
2 Tbsp soy sauce
1 tsp raw local honey
Juice of ½ lime

Drain the pickling liquor from the radishes and bring it to a boil in a small pan. In batches, drop the prepared squid into the boiling liquor 45 seconds only. Remove with a slotted spoon and let cool.

Cut the pickled radishes in half from top to tail. Mix all the ingredients for the dressing together.

Mix the squid, radishes, and cucumber with the cilantro. Toss with the dressing, season, and serve.

STORAGE The pickled radishes will last 2 weeks in a sterilized jar. The pickled squid will keep for one week in the refrigerator, submerged in the pickling liquor. Make the salad just before eating.

COOK NATURAL It's important to know how to sterilize containers, so you can make the most of your seasonal gluts by preserving them. Choose glass jars with tight-fitting lids and give them a really good clean with hot soapy water. Put them in the oven upside down so they can dry. Set the oven to 300°F [150°C]. When it reaches temperature, turn the oven off. Meanwhile, sterilize the lids (or rubber seals, if using Kilner jars) by boiling them in a saucepan 5 minutes. Leave the jars in the oven and the lids in the boiling water until you are ready to use them. Then fill warm jars with the hot preserves, dry the lids with a clean cloth, and fix them on tightly.

EATING SUMMER

apricots
artichokes
beets
bell peppers
broccoli
carrots
chard
cherries
cucumber
eggplants
fava beans
fennel
garlic
gooseberries
green beans and string beans
kohlrabi
mushrooms (cultivated)
new potatoes
onions and shallots
peas
potatoes (main crop)
radishes
raspberries
redcurrants (and blackcurrants and whitecurrants)
salad leaves
spinach
scallions
sweetcorn
strawberries
tomatoes
turnips and swedes
watercress
zucchini

Eating STRAWBERRIES

RAW
strawberries with mint and black pepper

MACERATED
strawberries with grappa

Strawberry **JAM**

Seafood salad with strawberries

Summer pudding

Strawberry ripple mascarpone ice cream

June to August/September A strawberry ripened to perfection is a cosmic experience for which we all feel a certain nostalgia. The zing and tingle in the mouth, buzzing with flavor, and then that divine sweetness that makes your eyes close with pleasure. A little less ripe, and strawberries actually have a savory twang that opens up a whole new repertoire of dishes to which they can be added. Try dotting them into salads, even seafood salads (see page 58).

Strawberries that are grown for local sale don't need to be hardy for transport. So the farmer can concentrate on growing more flavorful varieties that can be picked ripe and are therefore sweeter than most commercially grown strawberries. Also, strawberries can show a high level of pesticide residues, so buy organic if possible.

To keep strawberries fresh for longer, store them in the refrigerator in the punnet they came in, first removing any moldy or bruised berries as they will turn the rest. Don't wash the strawberries until you want to serve them, as they will retain water and become soggy. Remove them from the refrigerator 1 hour before you eat them, so they have a chance to warm up and become as sweet and aromatic as possible.

Strawberry jam

Strawberries at the height of summer are cheap. Take advantage of this abundance by making your own jam and preserving their sweetness for the winter. Slightly underripe strawberries make the best-tasting jam. Makes one 1⅛ lb [500 g] jar.

1⅛ lb [500 g] strawberries, juice of ½ lemon, 2¼ cups [450 g] jam sugar

Put a plate in the freezer. Pull off and discard the green stalks of the strawberries (I tend not to cut them out, to avoid waste). Mash half of them with a potato masher and cut the other half into quarters. Put all the berries into a small saucepan and squeeze in the lemon juice. Add the empty lemon shell along with the sugar, then place over medium heat and bring to a boil. Keep on a low boil 15 minutes, then test the jam to see if it is ready: take the plate from the freezer, put 1 tsp of the jam on top, and return to the freezer 2 minutes. Take the plate and turn it on its side. If the jam doesn't run, but wrinkles, it is ready. If not, test again 5 minutes later. Repeat if necessary. Meanwhile, sterilize a glass jar (see page 52). Fill the hot jar with the hot jam, seal, and let cool.

MORE STRAWBERRY JAM . . . AND LEFTOVERS
Jam tarts. Make Shortcrust pastry (see page 28) and use it to line tartlet cases. Preheat the oven to 350°F [180°C]. Fill each case two-thirds full with jam and bake 15 to 20 minutes.

Strawberry fool. To make a quick fool, whip 7 Tbsp [100 ml] heavy cream to soft peaks. Fold in 14 Tbsp [200 ml] live natural yogurt and 5¼ oz [150 g] Strawberry jam. Serves 4.

Strawberry ripple mascarpone ice cream

No ice-cream machine necessary. This is a very easy recipe to make. If you don't have time to make your own jam, store-bought will do fine. Serves 6 to 8.

7 oz [200 g] Strawberry jam
8¾ oz [250 g] mascarpone
⅝ cup [150 ml] heavy cream

Mix the mascarpone into the cream and whip the mixture until it forms stiff peaks.

Pour into a large freezer-proof container and put in the freezer. Remove after 1 hour and stir, then return to the freezer. After another hour, remove and stir in the strawberry jam with just a couple of turns, to create a ripple effect. Repeat this stirring process 2 or 3 more times, stirring just a little in order to keep the ripples of strawberry jam, until almost set.

Remove from the freezer 10 minutes before serving. Use a spoon dipped in boiling water as a scoop.

STORAGE Jam will keep sealed 1 year; once opened, eat within 1 month. Ice cream will keep in the freezer 1 month.

COOK NATURAL Making jams and preserves is a time-old tradition for preserving gluts of fresh produce. Make the most of seasonal fruit and veg and buy in bulk while it is cheap, preserving it whenever you can. Pectin is a natural setting agent that occurs in some fruits, mostly in the rinds and pips. It is extracted and sold in a powder form, or mixed into jam sugar. If you don't want to use white jam sugar, then buy the powder, or make your own liquid pectin using apple peelings and cores (see page 113), and use raw cane sugar—or another less processed sugar—instead.

Raw strawberries with mint and black pepper

Strawberries work surprisingly well with black pepper. Although sweet, the berries have a fresh vegetable note that holds the heat of the spice. Serves 2 as a dessert.

10½ oz [300 g] strawberries, 3 mint leaves, extra virgin olive oil (optional), aged balsamic vinegar (optional)

Pull off and discard the green tops of the strawberries. Cut the berries in half and place in a bowl. Sprinkle with freshly ground black pepper. Take the mint leaves, roll them up into a "cigar," cut into thin strips with a sharp knife, and sprinkle over the top. If you want to be really experimental, dress with a little extra virgin oil and balsamic vinegar.

MORE RAW STRAWBERRIES . . . AND LEFTOVERS
With goat's cheese and balsamic. Dress 1 quantity Raw strawberries with mint and black pepper with the balsamic vinegar and a crumble of your favorite goat's cheese. It tastes divine. Serves 2 as an appetizer or after-dinner savory.

Strawberry salsa. Make 1 quantity Raw strawberries with mint and black pepper, but quarter the strawberries. Add a little finely chopped red onion and cucumber. Serve with grilled chicken or fish, or in a burrito-style wrap. Serves 4 as a condiment.

Seafood salad with strawberries

This dish was an uncanny discovery, a match of unlikely ingredients that actually work really well together. A good extra virgin oil is important here; it unites the disparate flavors and gives the dish a lift. If you can't get hold of this particular variety of seafood, simply make up your own recipe, using what you have available. Try crab meat, cuttlefish, or even bream or bass fillets. Buy rope-grown mussels and diver-caught scallops, as conventional methods of gathering these shellfish can be harmful to the ocean floor. Serves 4 as an appetizer.

1 quantity Raw strawberries with mint and black pepper
14 Tbsp [200 ml] white wine
1 onion, halved
2 bay leaves (optional)
7 oz [200 g] rope-grown mussels
7 oz [200 g] cockles or clams
7 oz [200 g] squid, prepared weight
4 diver-caught scallops with their roes, cleaned
2 Tbsp extra virgin olive oil
Little Gem leaves and lemon wedges, to serve

First make a poaching broth for the seafood. Pour 3¼ cups [800 ml] water into a large saucepan and add the wine, onion, and bay leaves (if using). Bring to a boil, salting to taste, then reduce to a gentle simmer.

Meanwhile prepare the seafood, keeping each type separate as they will be cooked individually. Clean the mussels and remove their beards (the tassley bit of seaweed). Clean the cockles or clams. If any of the shellfish are open at this point, throw them away. Cut the squid into thin rings at the pointed end and into 1 in [3 cm] long strips where the body gets wider.

Cook the mussels in the broth 1 to 2 minutes until they open. Remove with a slotted spoon and put in a bowl. Return the broth to a boil and add the cockles or clams, cook 1 or 2 minutes, then remove and reserve with the mussels. Return the broth to a boil and cook the squid, scallops, and their roes 30 seconds, then remove. Set the broth aside, to serve after the salad.

Pick the mussels out of their shells, discarding any that have not opened. Pick the cockles. Halve the scallops. Mix all the seafood together with the strawberries, dress with the extra virgin oil, and serve on the leaves with lemon wedges. Serve the broth afterward, as a cleansing soup.

STORAGE This salad is best eaten fresh, but the cooked seafood and the broth will keep 3 or 4 days in a sealed container in the refrigerator. Return the seafood to room temperature to serve. Reheat the broth to boiling point before using. The raw strawberries should be eaten straightaway.

Macerated strawberries with grappa

I love the hint of alcohol and soft texture of macerated strawberries. They feel so decadent. Serves 2.

10½ oz [300 g] strawberries, 2 Tbsp grappa, 1 heaped tsp rapadura or raw cane sugar

Pull off and discard the green tops of the strawberries. Halve the berries and put them in a bowl with the grappa and sugar. Turn carefully and allow to macerate in the refrigerator 30 minutes, so all the juices begin to seep out and the strawberries soften. Turn now and again to recover them with the grappa juices. Serve in glasses with cream or crème fraîche.

MORE MACERATED STRAWBERRIES . . .
AND LEFTOVERS
Eton Mess. Leftover Macerated strawberries with grappa make a nice boozy version of Eton mess. Whip 3½ Tbsp [50 ml] heavy cream and fold in 2 Tbsp of the strawberries and some crushed meringues, if you have them. Serve in a wine glass. Serves 1.

Strawberry daiquiri. Blend 3½ oz [100 g] Macerated strawberries with grappa with a handful of ice and an extra 3½ Tbsp [50 ml] grappa. Makes 2.

Summer pudding

An all-time favorite of mine and so quick to make. I like to experiment with different fillings and fruits. This is best made the day before you want it, so the bread can soak up the juices and set. Serves 4 to 6.

1 quantity Macerated strawberries with grappa
7 oz [200 g] mixed summer fruits (not strawberries), such as raspberries, redcurrants, cherries, or blackberries
Juice of ½ lemon
3½ Tbsp [50 g] raw local honey, or to taste
4 to 6 x ⅜ in [1 cm] thick slices of sourdough or good white bread, crusts removed

Put the strawberries in a saucepan with the other fruits. Add the lemon juice, honey, and 3½ Tbsp [50 ml] water, taste, and add more honey if you would like it sweeter. Bring the fruits to a boil, then reduce the heat and simmer 2 minutes.

Line a 4½ cup [1 L] pudding basin with the slices of bread: place a disc of bread in the bottom, then run pieces up the sides, overlapping them slightly. Press the joins together to seal them, using a dab of water to help.

Fill the bread case with the summer fruits, reserving a few Tbsp of the juice. Cover the top with a circle of bread and seal it to the pudding's "walls." Place a small plate on top and put a weight on that; I use my mortar and pestle, but anything clean and heavy will do. Put it in the refrigerator.

The next day, carefully turn the pudding out on to a plate. Use the reserved juices to paint over the top to freshen it up and cover any white areas. Serve with plenty of fresh cream.

STORAGE The pudding will keep in its basin in the refrigerator 4 days. The macerated strawberries should be eaten immediately.

Eating FAVA BEANS

CHARGRILLED fava beans

RAW fava beans with mint

Chargrilled fava bean and crab bruschetta

Fava bean, pistachio, preserved lemon, and cilantro salad

SAUTÉED fava beans with mint and coriander

Fava bean and lamb pilaf

June to August Fava beans are a sure sign that summer is here. They begin small and sweet, raw and ready for salads; even the pods are tasty. As they grow larger and a become a little more bitter, I like to use them in Arabic pilafs (see page 67) and rustic Italian-style soups. Dried fava beans, make a sumptuous and moreish purée that, flavored with a squeeze of lemon juice and a pinch of salt, is better than any chickpea hummus.

Fava beans are hardy and easy to grow, even in poor soils. This means that they are readily available from local farmers. If you grow your own fava beans, you can also eat the small leaves by steaming or wilting them like spinach; you can even use the flowers to dress your salads.

Fava beans keep well in or out of the refrigerator, as they are well protected by their pods. If the pods become blemished, the beans will often still be perfect, so check inside before you throw them to the compost monster.

Raw fava beans with mint

When eating fava beans raw, pick the smaller pods as the beans will be that much sweeter. Allow 7 to 8¾ oz [200 to 250 g] per person, weighed in the pods. When podded, that should give you about 2 oz [60 g] each. Serves 2 as a side dish.

14 oz to 1⅛ lb [400 to 500 g] fava beans in their pods, extra virgin olive oil, 3 mint leaves, 1 red chili (optional)

Pop the beans from their pods. If the beans are larger, then peel off their skins as well to reveal the bright green bean inside, and compost the husks. (Avoid buying beans to eat raw late in the season, as they can be bitter.) Dress with extra virgin oil. Finely chop the mint and add it with salt and black pepper. Finely chop the chili and add that, too, if you like. Serve with fish, or as part of a cold lunch.

MORE RAW FAVA BEANS . . . AND LEFTOVERS
Quick preserved lemons. When you have too many lemons, use this recipe to preserve them another 2 or 3 weeks. Cut the lemons in half and squeeze the juice into a small saucepan. Cut the skins in half again and add to the pan. Add 5 tsp sea salt and a splash of water for each lemon. Bring to a boil with a lid on, then reduce the heat and steam 15 minutes until the lemon skins have softened. Sterilize a jar (see page 52). Fill the jar with the lemon skins and their salty juice and seal. If the lemon skins are not completely covered, squeeze enough extra lemon juice to cover them. To use, scrape out the remaining flesh from the skins and discard, then chop the rind finely.

Fattoush. Add any leftover Raw fava beans with mint to Fattoush (see page 88).

Fava bean tortilla. Add leftover Raw fava beans with mint to a Frittata (see page 40).

Fava bean, pistachio, preserved lemon, and cilantro salad

A big, vibrant salad that is full of flavor. Try making your own preserved lemons (see below left); it's quick and easy. Serves 4 as a side dish.

1 quantity Raw fava beans with mint
5 tsp red rice (optional)
3½ Tbsp [50 g] brown rice
3½ Tbsp [50 g] shelled pistachio nuts
½ preserved lemon, or Quick preserved lemon (see below left)
6 sprigs flat-leaf parsley, stalks finely chopped, leaves roughly chopped
6 sprigs cilantro, stalks finely chopped, leaves roughly chopped
Good glug of extra virgin olive oil

Slowly boil the red and brown rices in plenty of water until they are soft but still have bite when you try them; it should take about 35 minutes, but follow the packet instructions. If you are not using red rice, substitute brown rice instead, boiling a total of 2¾ oz [75 g]. Drain and rinse under cold water to cool the rice and remove some of the starch. Allow to drain in a sieve.

Toast the pistachio nuts under a hot grill, then crush slightly with a mortar and pestle or a rolling pin. Prepare the preserved lemon by scraping away the salty insides, then cutting the rind into long shreds.

Mix all the ingredients together with the extra virgin oil and season with salt and pepper.

STORAGE This salad will keep well in a sealed container in the refrigerator 3 days, but is better without the herbs. Return it to room temperature before eating. The raw fava beans should be eaten straightaway.

COOK NATURAL Fava beans are fresher when you buy them in the pod and this also gives you the bonus of the delicious pods, which can be used in various recipes. You can even eat them raw when they are small: try coating them in flour mixed with spices such as cumin, coriander, and a little salt. Deep-fry them, then dip them into seasoned yogurt or tahini, or add them to the salad above. The pods also add a great flavor to vegetable stock, so keep them in the freezer until you make a potful.

Chargrilled fava beans

I love cooking on the barbecue. This method is especially rewarding for fava beans, as you watch them cook straight on the hot coals as they steam in their own jackets. You can also cook these on a griddle pan. Serves 2 to 3 as a side dish.

1⅛ lb [500 g] fava beans

First light a barbecue or heat a griddle pan. If using a barbecue, allow the coals to become white hot and then to cool down a little. Place the fava beans in their pods directly on the coals, or on to the hot griddle. Allow about half of the skin to blacken and blister, then turn and allow the other side to char, too. After about 5 minutes, the beans will have steamed inside the pods. Once cool enough to handle, remove the beans from their pods.

MORE CHARGRILLED FAVA BEANS . . .
AND LEFTOVERS
Crab shell soup. If you have boiled your crab, place its shell in a large saucepan. (The shell of a chargrilled crab will not be suitable to make soup.) Add 1 chopped carrot, 1 chopped onion, and 1 chopped fennel bulb, cover with water, and simmer 2 hours. Strain the stock through a colander into a bowl. Remove any large claws and thick bits of shell. Return the rest of the shell and veg to the empty pan. Smash with a rolling pin to break it all up and return the stock. Stir and return to a boil, then pass everything through a sieve into a clean saucepan, pressing down to get as much of the crab goodness through the sieve as you can. Season and serve hot with crusty bread.

Chorizo with crab and fava beans. Barbecue some cooking chorizo, slice, and stir into the crab mixture before topping the bruschetta.

Chargrilled fava bean and crab bruschetta

Cooking crab on a barbecue intensifies its flavors and tastes so darn good! This is one of my favorites. If you don't have a barbecue, boil your crab instead. Serves 6 as an appetizer.

1 quantity **Chargrilled fava beans**
1 live crab (about 1kg+)
3 sprigs flat-leaf parsley, stalks finely chopped, leaves roughly chopped
Juice of ½ lemon
6 slices of sourdough bread, or baguette

1 garlic clove
Extra virgin olive oil

Light the barbecue if you have one and allow the coals to become white hot, then to cool down a little.

Meanwhile, to kill the crab humanely, turn it on its back and lift the triangular- or wedge-shaped flap. Beneath it you will find a small hole roughly in the middle of the body. Firmly drive a small knife into the hole straight down until it meets the upper shell.

Place the crab shell-side down on the white-hot coals and leave 8 minutes. Flip the crab and leave another 8 minutes. Remove it from the barbecue and let cool 15 minutes.

If you're boiling the crab instead, cook it in a very large pan of salted water at a rolling boil, allowing crabs up to 2¼ lb [1 kg] 10 to 12 minutes, plus 3 or 4 minutes more for every extra 1⅛ lb [500 g].

To pick the crab meat, pull off the legs and claws. Crack them open with a rolling pin or pestle and pick out the meat with the handle of a teaspoon or a small knife. Now prize the main shell from the body. Discard the gills, which look like pointy fingers. Spoon the delicious brown meat from the shell. Cut the body in half with a heavy knife or cleaver and pick out the white meat from all the little crevices.

Mix all the brown and white crab meat with the fava beans, parsley, and lemon juice.

Toast the bread on the barbecue or in a griddle pan until it colors slightly on both sides. Rub with garlic and extra virgin oil and top with the crab mixture.

STORAGE The bruschetta is best eaten immediately, but the crab topping mixture and the chargrilled fava beans will keep 3 days in sealed containers in the refrigerator. Return both to room temperature to serve.

Sautéed fava beans with mint and coriander

Fava beans are great sautéed and have an Arabic feel here, with spices and mint. Serves 2 to 3 as a side dish, or as part of a mixed meze.

1⅛ lb [500 g] fava beans in their pods, glug of light olive oil, 1 garlic clove, 3 mint leaves, pinch of coriander seeds, juice of ¼ lemon

Remove the beans from their pods. Heat a skillet with a lid over medium heat with the light olive oil. Gently fry the beans. Slice the garlic and add to the pan, cover, and cook 2 minutes. Chop the mint leaves. Remove the lid, add the chopped mint, coriander, and lemon juice and fry a further 2 minutes.

MORE SAUTÉED FAVA BEANS . . . AND LEFTOVERS
Minestrone. Any leftover Sautéed fava beans with mint and coriander are delicious added to Minestrone (see page 69).

Pilaf salad. Eat the pilaf cold the next day, freshening up the flavors with crushed nuts, pomegranate seeds, and chopped parsley, adding a squeeze of lemon juice and more salt and pepper if you want.

Fava bean and lamb pilaf

Pilaf is a delicious and aromatic Middle Eastern dish made from rice cooked in a rich broth of onions and spices. It is from the same family as Indian pilau or biryani and great to cook at home, because it's such a simple, marvellous one-pot wonder. Serves 4.

1 quantity Sautéed fava beans with mint and coriander
7 oz [200 g] lamb, either leftover from a roast, or raw neck fillet
Glug of light olive oil
2 onions, sliced
1 Tbsp ground coriander
3 garlic cloves, roughly chopped
5¼ oz [150 g] brown basmati rice
Small cinnamon stick
Yogurt, toasted cumin seeds, and extra virgin olive oil, to serve

Preheat the oven to 325°F [160°C]. If using leftover roast lamb, shred it into bite-size pieces. If using a neck fillet, season it, sear it on all sides in the light olive oil, then put it in the oven 15 minutes to cook through. Cut it into shreds.

Meanwhile, in a heavy-based casserole dish, gently fry the onions in light olive oil 15 to 20 minutes, until they are soft and caramelized. Add the coriander and garlic and fry a further 2 minutes.

Add the rice and stir, coating every grain with oil, onion, and spice. Add the lamb, fava beans, cinnamon, and 1⅞ cups [450 ml] water. Bring to a boil, then reduce the heat, taste, and adjust the seasoning. Put the lid on and place the dish in the oven about 45 minutes. All the water should be absorbed.

Serve with yogurt seasoned with toasted cumin seeds, salt and pepper, and extra virgin oil.

STORAGE Pilaf will keep really well 3 days in a sealed container in the refrigerator. It's delicious cold or reheated, or even at room temperature. To reheat it, put in a covered ovenproof dish with a splash of water to loosen, then put in an oven preheated to 350°F [180°C] 20 minutes, or until piping hot right through. Sautéed fava beans will keep in a sealed container in the refrigerator 3 days. Reheat in a sauté pan, with extra oil if you need it.

Raw zucchini "spaghetti"

Eat this simply as it is, or use it as a substitute for pasta and dress with tomato sauce and parmesan. Serves 2 as a side dish.

7 oz [200 g] zucchini, extra virgin olive oil

For this recipe, pick the very freshest, crispest zucchini. Wash them, take a box grater, and turn it on its side. Run the zucchini along the grater, creating long strings of it. Keep going until the zucchini loses its rigidity, then finely slice the leftover piece with a knife. Place the zucchini in a bowl and dress with extra virgin oil, salt, and pepper.

MORE RAW ZUCCHINI . . . AND LEFTOVERS
Zucchini "spaghetti" with almonds. Soak 3½ Tbsp [50 g] almonds, overnight, if possible. This will make them more digestible and take on a nice water-chestnut-like crunch. Add them to 1 quantity Raw zucchini "spaghetti" with a squeeze of lemon juice and a sprinkling of roughly chopped parsley. Add a sprinkle of cayenne pepper, if you like. Serves 2 as a side dish.

Tempura. Raw zucchini "spaghetti" is a good candidate for the tempura treatment. Make it in the same way as Tempura of broccoli (see page 31) and serve with sweet chili sauce.

Zucchini and feta fritters with yogurt

These are a wonderful Greek classic. They are easy to make, incredibly moreish, and keep well, so can be made ahead, then reheated. Serves 4 as an appetizer.

1 quantity Raw zucchini "spaghetti,"
  prepared but not dressed with extra virgin oil
1 scallion, finely sliced
3 sprigs of dill, chopped
9 mint leaves, roughly chopped
2½ oz [70 g] feta, crumbled
1 small egg, lightly beaten
2 Tbsp all-purpose flour
6 zucchini flowers (optional)
Light olive oil
⅓ cup [80 ml] Greek yogurt, to serve

Spread the zucchini spaghetti on a clean dish towel and leave 5 minutes, then fold the dish towel on top and pat it dry.

Transfer to a bowl and add the rest of the ingredients, except the zucchini flowers (if using), oil, and yogurt.

Mix well and season with pepper; you probably won't need much (if any) salt, as the feta is salty. If you have zucchini flowers, stuff them with some of the mixture.

Put a heavy-based skillet over medium heat with a glug of light olive oil. Drop a small piece of the zucchini mixture into the pan to test if it is hot enough: when it sizzles, the pan is at the right temperature.

First, fry the stuffed zucchini flowers, if you have them. Then drop large Tbsp of the rest of the mixture into the pan. Whether cooking flowers or fritters, allow them to color to a light brown on one side, then flip and color on the other.

When cooked, remove from the pan and rest on a clean dish towel or paper towels to absorb excess oil.

Serve with Greek yogurt, or make tzatziki by adding a little finely chopped cucumber, crushed garlic, extra virgin oil, lemon juice, and seasoning.

STORAGE Zucchini fritters will keep in a sealed container in the refrigerator 3 days. Reheat them in an oven preheated to 350°F [180°C] until hot right through. The zucchini "spaghetti" is best eaten immediately, but will keep 2 days in a sealed container in the refrigerator.

Chargrilled zucchini

You can make these either on a barbecue or in a griddle pan, and they taste great hot or cold. Serves 2 as a side dish.

5¾ oz [160 g] zucchini, light olive oil

Cut the zucchini into lengthwise slices about ⅜ in [1 cm] thick. Light a barbecue and allow the charcoals to turn white hot, then cool down a little, or heat a griddle pan on the stovetop. Toss the zucchini slices in light olive oil. Place them on the barbecue or griddle side by side, but don't layer them on top of each other or they will sweat rather than char. After 2 to 5 minutes, they should be charred on one side. Flip over and char equally on the other side. Season with salt and pepper and serve.

MORE CHARGRILLED ZUCCHINI . . .

AND LEFTOVERS
Tagliatelle with chargrilled veggies and mozzarella. Leftover Grilled salad makes a great pasta topping. I particularly like it with spelt pasta.

Frittata. Add 4 lightly beaten eggs to leftover cooled Grilled salad and fry gently in light olive oil in an ovenproof skillet 10 minutes. Finish under a hot grill until the eggs are just set, but don't overcook. Serves 2 to 4.

Grilled salad of zucchini, radicchio, basil, and mozzarella

Chargrilled veggies are just delicious and replace the need for meat with their robust flavor and savoriness. If you can't find za'atar, try making the spice mix yourself with dried oregano and thyme ground in a mortar and pestle with some sesame seeds, salt, and a pinch of sumac. Serves 4 to 6.

1 quantity Chargrilled zucchini
1 red onion, cut into thin wedges
½ head of radicchio (about 5¾ oz [160 g]), cut into thinnish wedges, with core attached
2 Tbsp light olive oil
4¼ oz [120 g] buffalo mozzarella
Extra virgin olive oil
Couple of pinches of za'atar
3½ oz [100 g] black olives, pitted
Finely grated zest of ½ unwaxed lemon
10 basil leaves

Toss the red onion and radicchio in the light olive oil and grill in the same way as the zucchini (see left).

Arrange all the grilled vegetables on a platter. Tear the mozzarella into bite-size pieces, dropping them evenly on to the plate.

Dress with a drizzle of extra virgin oil and a sprinkle of za'atar, scatter with the olives, and add the lemon zest and basil leaves.

STORAGE This salad and the chargrilled zucchini will keep well in a sealed container in the refrigerator 3 days. Return both to room temperature to serve.

COOK NATURAL Zucchini grow brilliantly in a temperate climate and inevitably leave us with a glut of oversized zucchini and marrows. If growing your own, share your wealth with friends. Or, to preserve them, you can pack chargrilled zucchini into sterilized jars (see page 52), cover with oil, and keep in the refrigerator a couple of weeks, or make a chutney with marrows (for the method, see page 87).

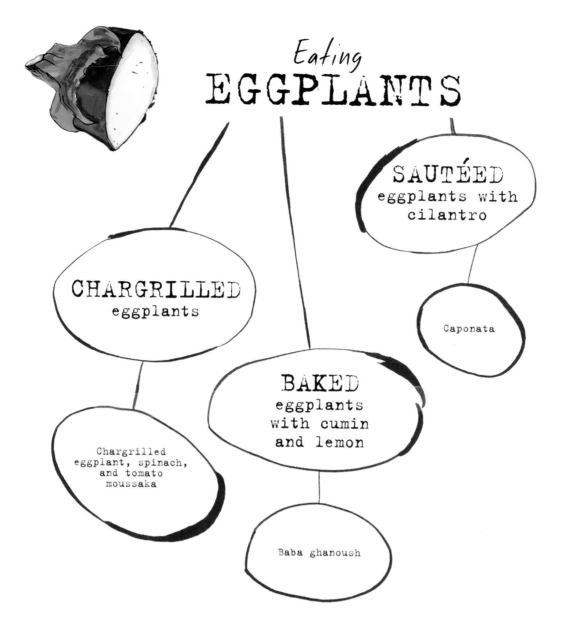

Eating
EGGPLANTS

CHARGRILLED eggplants

Chargrilled eggplant, spinach, and tomato moussaka

BAKED eggplants with cumin and lemon

Baba ghanoush

SAUTÉED eggplants with cilantro

Caponata

July to October The eggplant is a king among vegetables, bulbous in its purple cloak and green crown. Once cooked, it becomes a rich and buttery delicacy, the caviar of the veg patch and to be enjoyed as such.

My favorite way to eat it is cooked on a chargrill, either sliced and given a lick of olive oil then charred, or simply placed whole in the coals to bake in its skin, allowing the juices to sweeten and the flesh to become smoky and velvety smooth. Sautéed eggplants caramelize quickly and become tasty little morsels.

I've included three classic recipes, each with their own twist. Baba ghanoush (see page 77) is top of my list. Rich and silky in texture, I like to add a little yogurt to lighten the delicious, creamy dip. Caponata (see right) is also a must for this time of year, with tomatoes ripe on the vines and basil flourishing. Moussaka (see page 78) is a special dish, good to make on a Sunday when you've got some time on your hands.

Eggplants keep best in the refrigerator.

Sautéed eggplants with cilantro

Sprinkle these on to a green salad and add a tahini dressing, or stir them into a tomato or Bolognese sauce to serve with pasta, or just eat on the side. Serves 4 as a side dish.

1 eggplant (about 8¾ to 10½ oz [250 to 300 g]), good glug of light olive oil, squeeze of lemon juice, 6 sprigs cilantro

Cut the eggplant into ⅜ to ¾ in [1 to 2 cm] cubes. Heat a large skillet with the light olive oil until hot. Add the eggplant cubes in batches, sautéing on all sides until they are browned. Season with salt, pepper, and lemon juice. Chop the cilantro. Drain the eggplant on paper towels to blot excess oil, then serve warm or at room temperature with the chopped cilantro.

MORE SAUTÉED EGGPLANTS . . . AND LEFTOVERS
Peperonata. If you have lots of bell peppers, substitute the eggplant in the Caponata for bell peppers and cook in the same way.

Stuffed tomatoes. If you have some nice big tomatoes, cut them in half and hollow them out. Preheat the oven to 350°F [180°C]. Fill the tomato shells with Caponata, made using the hollowed-out tomato flesh and seeds if possible, and roast in the oven 25 minutes.

Caponata

A summer treat, this dish bursts with sunshine from all the flavor of tomato and eggplant. Delicious eaten as an appetizer with bread, or turned into a pasta sauce. Serves 6 as a side dish or appetizer.

1 quantity Sautéed eggplants with cilantro
2 celery sticks, including leaves, finely chopped
Glug of light olive oil
1 garlic clove, roughly chopped
3½ oz [100 g] Stewed tomatoes with garlic and oregano (see page 87)
3½ Tbsp [50 g] capers (salted are best), rinsed
1 Tbsp red or white wine vinegar
1 heaped tsp rapadura or raw cane sugar
4 sprigs parsley, stalks finely chopped, leaves roughly chopped

Fry the celery in the light olive oil in a saucepan 5 minutes. Add the garlic and fry 1 minute.

Add the eggplants, tomatoes, capers, vinegar, and sugar. Bring to a boil and simmer 10 minutes.

Serve hot or at room temperature, sprinkled with the parsley. If serving cold, let cool before adding the herb, to keep it fresh and green.

STORAGE Caponata is like a stew, so it's even better after a day or 2 and will keep in a sealed container in the refrigerator 4 or 5 days. Reheat gently in a saucepan to serve, adding a splash of water if needed. Sautéed eggplants will keep in a sealed container in the refrigerator, without the cilantro, 3 days. Reheat quickly in a sauté pan with a dash more oil, if needed, to serve.

Baked eggplants with cumin and lemon

A simple way to prepare eggplants, these taste amazing turned into a pasta sauce, or eaten as an antipasti with rare beef, or even just spread on toasts. Serves 6 as a side dish or dip.

2 eggplants (about 1⅛ lb [500 g]), pinch of cumin seeds, juice of ¼ lemon

You can cook these on a barbecue, a griddle pan, or an open flame. If using a barbecue, get it to the stage of glowing white coals, then let cool a little. If using a griddle or a flame, place the griddle over high heat, or just turn your gas flame on, and preheat the oven to 340°F [170°C]. Now char the eggplants whole, turning with tongs to allow each side to blacken. If using a barbecue, after charring the eggplants on high heat, move them to a cooler part of the grill to cook through 20 to 30 minutes, until soft right to the center. If using a griddle or gas flame, once charred, bake the eggplants in the hot oven 30 to 40 minutes. Whichever method you use, make sure your eggplant is completely soft. Let cool a little, then scrape out all the flesh into a bowl. Discard the burned skin. Season, mix with the cumin seeds and lemon juice, and serve as a salad, side dish, or dip.

MORE BAKED EGGPLANTS . . . AND LEFTOVERS
With chermoula. Cook 1 quantity Baked eggplants, but don't scrape the flesh out or add the cumin or lemon. Meanwhile, make 1 quantity Chermoula (see page 27). Cut the Baked eggplants into halves. Spread a good dollop of chermoula on each half and serve hot or cold. Serves 4 as an appetizer or side dish.

With venison carpaccio. Thinly slice raw venison fillet steak and arrange on a plate with blobs of leftover Baba ghanoush. Dress carefully with lemon juice and extra virgin oil.

Baba ghanoush

One of my favorite recipes of all time. This must have a smokiness to it and that is created while scorching the eggplants. Often the dip is intensely rich and creamy; this is a lighter version that uses yogurt. Serves 4 to 6 as an appetizer or part of a mixed meze.

1 quantity Baked eggplants with cumin and lemon
½ slice of stale bread
1 garlic clove, grated
1½ Tbsp thick live natural yogurt, or to taste
Good glug of extra virgin olive oil, or to taste
Juice of ½ lemon, or to taste
Pinch cumin seeds, or to taste
A few sprigs of cilantro or parsley, roughly chopped

Chop the eggplant flesh by hand until it is almost a purée, but still has some texture.

Soak the bread in water a few seconds until it is soft, then squeeze it dry. Crumble into the eggplant.

Now add the rest of the ingredients, mix, and season, then adjust the flavors to your taste. I like a lot of lemon; you might prefer more yogurt, oil, or cumin.

Serve in a bowl, with flatbread on the side, as an appetizer or part of a meze.

STORAGE Baba ghanoush and baked eggplants keep well 4 days in sealed containers in the refrigerator. Return both to room temperature to serve.

Chargrilled eggplants

The scorched flesh of an eggplant is exquisite in taste. It reminds me of eating in Morocco, where it was served up on plates with fried fish and lemon. Eggplants take a while to cook, so you don't want the barbecue or griddle to be at searing heat; you will need to adjust the temperature as you cook, so they become tender all the way through. Serves 5 to 6 as a side dish.

2 eggplants (about 1⅛ lb [500 g]), light olive oil

If using a barbecue, allow the coals to become white hot, then to cool down a little. Or put a griddle pan over medium heat. Slice the eggplants into ⅜ in [1 cm] thick slices from top to tail. Brush them with light olive oil and season with salt. Put on the barbecue or griddle pan and allow to char, brushing with more oil as they cook; eggplants are best when they are slightly burned in places and golden in others. Once charred, flip and char the other side. Check they are soft and cooked through. Serve hot or cold.

MORE CHARGRILLED EGGPLANTS . . .
AND LEFTOVERS
Rolled with anchovy and piquillo. As a little snack, cut leftover chargrilled eggplant slices into quarters and roll each one with a piquillo pepper and an anchovy inside, securing shut with a cocktail stick. Great as a predinner amuse-bouche.

Mixed grill salad. My favorite salad: a simple mix of whatever vegetables are available, chargrilled, seasoned with a little yogurt and a sprinkle of sumac, cumin, and/or chili.

Chargrilled eggplant, spinach, and tomato moussaka

A vegetarian moussaka full of flavor and sustenance. If you prefer meat, add 7 oz [200 g] sautéed ground lamb to the recipe instead of the lentils. Serves 4 to 6.

1 quantity Chargrilled eggplants
1 onion, thinly sliced
Glug of light olive oil
½ tsp cumin seeds
3½ oz [100 g] Puy lentils
1¾ lb [800 g] Stewed tomatoes with garlic and
    oregano (see page 87) or 1½ x 14 oz [400 g] cans
    chopped tomatoes
7 oz [200 g] spinach or chard, stalks finely chopped, leaves
    roughly chopped
5¼ oz [150 g] ricotta
⅝ cup [150 ml] live natural yogurt
Pinch grated nutmeg

In a large pan, fry the onion slowly in the light olive oil with the cumin. Meanwhile, simmer the lentils 15 to 25 minutes until tender, then drain.

Preheat the oven to 375°F [190°C]. Add the tomatoes to the onion, bring to a boil and add the lentils, then the spinach or chard. As soon as the leaves wilt, remove from the heat. In a bowl, mix the ricotta and yogurt and season with salt and pepper.

In an ovenproof dish, layer half the lentil mixture, half the eggplant, then half the yogurt mixture, adding a grating of nutmeg. Then repeat the layers, finishing with the yogurt mixture and another grating of nutmeg. Bake in the oven 25 minutes, until hot right through.

STORAGE Moussaka keeps well in the refrigerator 4 days. In fact it's better the day after cooking, as the flavors merge and it sets a little more firmly. Cover and reheat in an oven preheated to 350°F [180°C] until hot right through. Chargrilled eggplants will keep 4 days in a sealed container in the refrigerator. Return to room temperature before serving.

COOK NATURAL Eating less meat is good for our health and the environment. I find that some veggies and legumes satisfy my cravings for meat, such as the addition of lentils to the veggie moussaka above. Eat vegetables that are high in protein and iron such as chickpeas, lentils, beans and other legumes, kale, spinach, and winter greens to make sure you are getting all the vitamins and minerals you need. Restaurants often save money by cooking with less meat. This is easy to do at home, too: you only need about 3½ oz [100 g] meat per person in stews, padded out with legumes or "meaty" vegetables such as eggplants, When serving a fillet of meat, 5¼ oz [150 g] per person is a good guideline for portion size.

Eating
APRICOTS

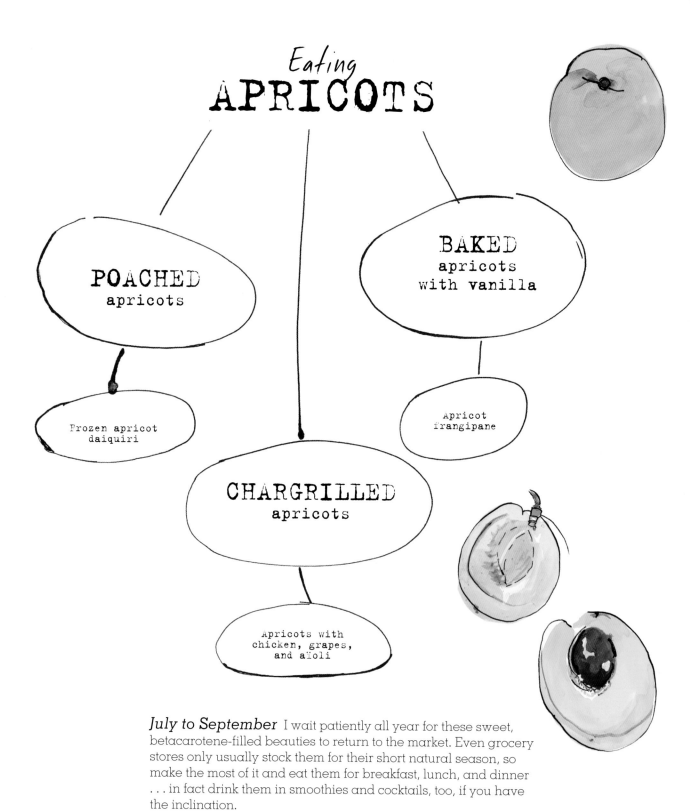

POACHED
apricots

Frozen apricot
daiquiri

BAKED
apricots
with **vanilla**

Apricot
frangipane

CHARGRILLED
apricots

Apricots with
chicken, grapes,
and aïoli

July to September I wait patiently all year for these sweet, betacarotene-filled beauties to return to the market. Even grocery stores only usually stock them for their short natural season, so make the most of it and eat them for breakfast, lunch, and dinner . . . in fact drink them in smoothies and cocktails, too, if you have the inclination.

You must choose your fruit wisely, as some that were picked too early will never sweeten and will have a dry, woolly texture that is utterly disappointing compared to the almondy sweet, butterscotch juiciness of a ripe fruit. Choose apricots that are slightly soft, but still firm, with a good strong color and mild aroma. They should be relatively heavy for their size, indicating the weight of juice within.

All stone fruits can contain high pesticide residues, so buy organic if possible. Keep them in the refrigerator as soon as they are ripe to lengthen their life, but return them to room temperature before eating for the best flavor and aroma.

Chargrilled apricots

Serve with breakfast as a real treat, or just with some crème fraîche as a quick dessert. Fabulously delicious and easy! Serves 2.

About 7 oz [200 g] apricots, 5 Tbsp [75 g] rapadura or raw cane sugar

Heat a griddle pan, skillet, or heavy-based skillet over medium-high heat. Meanwhile, halve the apricots, twist each half and pull it apart, then remove the stones. Sprinkle the sugar on to a plate and place the apricot halves cut-side down in it. When the griddle is hot, put the apricots on it, sugar-side down. Allow the fruits to become caramelized, then flip them over to char on the other side. The sugar will burn a little, but don't worry, it tastes amazing.

MORE CHARGRILLED APRICOTS . . .
AND LEFTOVERS
Ensalada Rusa. If you have leftover aïoli, boil 3½ oz [100 g] finely chopped potatoes with 3½ oz [100 g] finely chopped carrots until tender, then drain. Boil 3½ Tbsp [50 g] peas 3 minutes, then drain. Hard-boil 2 eggs, peel them, then finely chop. If you have it, add a finely chopped red bell pepper, too. Mix everything with 2 heaped Tbsp aïoli. Serves 4 as a side dish.

With ricotta on toast. Serve 1 quantity Chargrilled apricots on a slice of sourdough toast with a spoon each of ricotta and raw honey. This is outstanding for breakfast, or makes an interesting dessert. Serves 2.

Apricots with chicken, grapes, and aïoli

A great, summery salad. The bittersweet apricots make this off-the-wall version of the British classic coronation chicken into something really special. Serves 4 as an appetizer.

For the salad
1 quantity Chargrilled apricots
2 chicken legs
Drizzle of light olive oil
1 tsp curry powder
12 grapes, halved
3 sprigs cilantro, stalks finely chopped, leaves roughly chopped
1 Little Gem, washed, leaves separated

For the aïoli
1 egg
3 garlic cloves
⅝ cup [150 ml] extra virgin olive oil

Preheat the oven to 350°F [180°C]. Dress the chicken with the light olive oil, curry powder, salt, and pepper, then put it on a small baking sheet and roast in the oven 35 to 40 minutes until cooked right through. Check by piercing the largest piece to the bone; the juices should run clear. If there is any trace of pink, cook a few minutes more, then test again. Let cool enough to handle, then shred into large pieces. Reserve the curry-flavored oil from the sheet.

Now make the aïoli. Place the egg and garlic in a blender with a pinch of salt and pepper. Turn it on, then pour in the extra virgin oil in a very slow trickle, until thick and emulsified. If it splits, remove from the blender, add a new egg yolk to the blender, then slowly pour the split mixture on to it, while blitzing. Store in a jar in the refrigerator.

Put the shredded chicken into a bowl, mix in the curry oil from the sheet and 2 heaped Tbsp of aïoli. Add the grapes, cilantro, lettuce leaves, and chargrilled apricots. Turn just 2 or 3 times to mix, but leave all the ingredients with their bright colors. Serve on small plates.

STORAGE The chargrilled apricots, aïoli, and chicken will keep, separately, 3 days in sealed containers in the refrigerator. Return them all to room temperature before serving.

Baked apricots with vanilla

These are deliciously fragrant. I love eating them for breakfast with yogurt, or serving them as a light dessert after a rich meal. Serves 5 to 6.

1⅛ lb [500 g] apricots, ¾ cup [150 g] rapadura or raw cane sugar, 1 vanilla pod or 1 tsp vanilla extract, a little butter

Preheat the oven to 350°F [180°C]. Halve the apricots, twist each half and pull it apart, then remove the stones. Lay on a baking sheet and sprinkle with the sugar and vanilla extract (if using). Toss everything with your hands, ending with the apricots hollow-side up. Split the vanilla pod (if using) down its length with a knife, scrape out the seeds, and add them to the hollows. Throw in the pod, then put a piece of butter on each fruit. Bake 15 minutes, until the sugar has melted and the fruits are soft.

MORE BAKED APRICOTS . . . AND LEFTOVERS
Apricot jam. Mash 1 quantity Baked apricots with vanilla with a fork and put in a clean pot up to 1 week in the refrigerator. Serve on sourdough toast.

Apricot clafoutis. Preheat the oven to 350°F [180°C]. Butter an 8 in [20 cm] round earthenware dish and dust all sides with rapadura or raw cane sugar. Mix ¾ cup [100 g] spelt flour with 3 large, lightly beaten eggs, ½ cup [100 g] rapadura or raw cane sugar, and a drop of vanilla extract, then whisk in ⅝ cup [150 ml] milk, ¾ cup [170 ml] heavy cream, and 3½ Tbsp [50 g] melted butter. Mix in 1 quantity Baked apricots with vanilla and pour into the dish; it should be two-thirds full. Bake about 30 minutes, until it is set. Serve warm or cold with cream. Serves 4.

Apricot frangipane

Frangipane is just about my favorite dessert-cake-whatever. The rich almond sponge has all the flavor and moistness that a flour-based sponge lacks, and frangipane is a good carrier for tart seasonal fruits. At my restaurant we put a different frangipane on the menu each season, from quinces to rhubarb. Makes about 12 portions.

For the filling
1 quantity Baked apricots with vanilla
3½ oz [100 g] ground almonds
½ cup [100 g] rapadura or raw cane sugar
7 Tbsp [100 g] unsalted butter, slightly softened
1 large egg, lightly beaten

For the rough puff pastry
2 cups [250 g] spelt or all-purpose flour, plus more to dust
⅞ cup [190 g] cold butter, cut into ⅜ in [1 cm] cubes
½ cup [125 ml] cold water

Start with the pastry: put the flour in a bowl, add the butter and stir, then mix in the water until it comes together as a dough. Roll out into a large rectangle on a lightly floured surface. Fold over one short side of the dough by one-third of the rectangle's length, then fold the other short side by one-third over the top. Give the folded pastry a quarter turn. Roll out the sheet again, then repeat the folding. Place in a clean plastic bag and chill 30 minutes.

Meanwhile, mix all the ingredients for the filling except the apricots and beat until smooth. Preheat the oven to 350°F [180°C].

On a lightly floured surface, roll out the rough puff pastry to ¹⁄₁₆ to ¼ in [3 to 5 mm] thick. Use the pastry to line a 8 x 12 in [20 x 30 cm] deep baking sheet. Using a knife, score a border into the pastry ¾ to 1 in [2 to 3 cm] from the edge.

Spread the frangipane mixture evenly over the pastry in a layer about ⅜ in [1 cm] thick, up to the border but not over it. Put the apricots on top. Bake in the oven 25 to 30 minutes until both the pastry and frangipane have risen and are golden.

STORAGE The apricots will keep 1 week and the tart 3 days in the refrigerator in sealed containers. Return both to room temperature to serve. Any spare rough puff pastry will freeze well.

Passata

Preserve an abundance of tomatoes with this recipe . . . or just make a nice tomato sauce! Makes one 1⅛ lb [500 g] jar.

2¼ lb [1 kg] ripe tomatoes, 2 to 3 basil leaves

Wash the tomatoes, then blend them to a fine pulp. Gently simmer them in a wide saucepan 15 to 30 minutes, until they have reduced to a thick sauce. Taste them as they reduce, decide when you have reached your desired consistency and flavor, then stop cooking. Sterilize a 1⅛ lb [500 g] jar (see page 52), put the basil leaves at the bottom and fill with the passata.

MORE PASSATA . . . AND LEFTOVERS

Harira. Finely chop 1 red onion and 1 celery stick with its leaves. Gently fry both 10 minutes in a little light olive oil with ½ tsp each of cumin seeds, paprika, turmeric, ground ginger, cinnamon, and a pinch of salt. Now pour in 3½ Tbsp [50 g] green lentils, 4¼ oz [120 g] cooked chickpeas, 10½ oz [300 g] Passata, and 2 cups [500 ml] water. Simmer 30 minutes. Finish the soup with a knob of butter and a sprig of chopped parsley and serve with lemon wedges. Serves 4 to 6.

Gnocchi. Passata makes a great instant sauce for gnocchi. Boil 2¼ lb [1 kg] Desiree potatoes 20 minutes, or until soft. Drain and, when cool enough to handle, peel off the skins and compost them. Mash the potato, season to taste, and add a small lightly beaten egg and 2⅓ cups [280 g] spelt flour. Knead. If it feels a bit wet, add a little more flour. Split the dough into 4. One at a time, dust each piece with flour and roll into a long sausage about ¾ in [2 cm] thick. Cut into 1 in [3 cm] long pieces, dust with flour, and cook immediately. To cook, drop into simmering water 5 minutes, or until the gnocchi float to the surface. Mix into hot Passata and sprinkle with finely grated parmesan. Serves 4 to 6.

Shakshuka

The best breakfast, a healthy yet hearty replacement for the fried version. We serve it in huge pans from my festival café, with hundreds of eggs poaching in the rich tomato sauce. Serves 2.

10½ oz [300 g] **Passata**
1 red onion, thinly sliced
½ tsp ground cumin
1 tsp sweet paprika
Glug of light olive oil
1 mild green chili, sliced on the diagonal (optional)
2 garlic cloves, roughly chopped
4 eggs
3 sprigs parsley or cilantro, roughly chopped

Gently fry the onion with the cumin and paprika in the light olive oil, adding a pinch of salt and half the chili, if using, 10 minutes, until soft. Add the garlic and fry a further 5 minutes.

Add the passata and simmer 10 minutes. If the sauce becomes too dry, add a little water.

When you're ready to eat, make four hollows in the sauce and crack in the eggs. Cover with a lid and simmer 5 minutes for soft yolks and 10 minutes for hard-cooked eggs. Serve, sprinkled with the herbs and a little pepper, on your favorite toast, or with bread. Sprinkle with the rest of the chili, if you like.

STORAGE The shakshuka will keep well in a sealed container in the refrigerator 4 days. The passata should keep at least 2 weeks in a sterilized jar (see page 52).

EATING FALL

apples, pears, and quince
artichokes
beets
bell peppers
broccoli
blackberries
cabbages
carrots
celery
celery root
chestnuts and cobnuts
eggplants
elderberries
fennel
garlic
Jerusalem artichokes
kale
kohlrabi
leeks
mushrooms (wild and cultivated)
onions and shallots
parsnips
plums and damsons
potatoes (main crop)
spinach
squashes and pumpkins
sweetcorn
tomatoes
turnips and rutabagas
zucchini

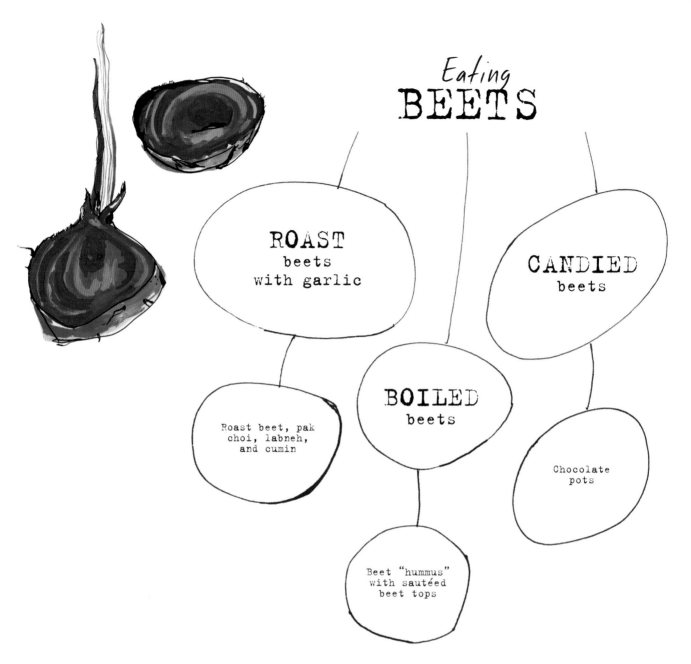

Eating BEETS

ROAST beets with garlic

CANDIED beets

BOILED beets

Roast beet, pak choi, labneh, and cumin

Chocolate pots

Beet "hummus" with sautéed beet tops

July to January Beet is a stout, rotund hero of the soil. When roasted, it is one of my favorite things. Candy sweet and sticky with a natural fruit molasses, it's no wonder that beet also works so well in desserts . . . try the Chocolate pots (see page 99), which marry monstrously dark chocolate with candied beet and its syrup. The outcome will have even the biggest beet skeptic begging for more.

The common deep red- or magenta-colored beet is gorgeous in its own right, but there are many interesting and beautiful varieties to be discovered, from candy stripes of white and red to golden, yellow, and pink.

Buy beets with fresh green leaves. The leaves taste good, are nutritious, and should always be eaten. They deteriorate more quickly than the root, so remove them when you get home, give them a good wash to remove any grit, and store in a bag in the refrigerator. Sauté these greens in the same way as chard or kale, adding spices and lemon for an exotic twist to a vegetable classic (see right). Wash them thoroughly, as they tend to harbor grit. The roots can be stored at room temperature.

Beets lose more than 25 percent of their folate when cooked; eating them raw will preserve this brain compound. I love them raw anyway, grated into salads with lots of nuts and seeds (see page 126), or finely sliced and used to dip into creamy goat's cheese or hummus.

Boiled beets

Very easy to prepare and a great snack to have in the refrigerator, ready to make into a number of delicious salads. Serves 4 as a side dish.

12¼ to 14 oz [350 to 400 g] beets, extra virgin olive oil (optional)

Wash the beets and remove the leaves. If the leaves are fresh, save them to use as greens (see right). Put the beets into a small saucepan and cover with plenty of water. Bring to a boil, then reduce the heat and simmer about 40 minutes, topping up the water if necessary (the beets should always be covered). Check the beets are soft by piercing them with a knife; it should meet no resistance. Drain and, when they are cool enough to handle, rub off the skins and cut off the rough tops. Slice and eat as they are—I like them like this—but dress with extra virgin oil and salt if you wish.

MORE BOILED BEETS . . . AND LEFTOVERS
Borscht. Make 1 quantity Boiled beets. When you drain them, keep the liquid. Rub the skin from the beets, quarter them, then blend in batches, covered with some of the cooking liquid, until smooth, adding extra liquid if necessary to make a thick soup. Season well with salt and pepper and a squeeze of lemon juice. Serves 2.

Beet nemesis. Preheat the oven to 150°C [300°F]. Line an 8 in [20 cm] round cake tin (a solid one, don't use a springform tin) with baking parchment and sit it in a large, deep baking sheet. Melt 6½ oz [180 g] dark chocolate with 9 Tbsp [125 g] butter. Beat 3 eggs with ⅞ cup [180 g] rapadura or raw cane sugar until tripled in volume. Purée 5¼ oz [150 g] Boiled beets. Fold all 3 mixtures together, pour into the tin, and bake 25 to 30 minutes. When the cake is set, remove it from the oven, let cool, then refrigerate. Slice and serve with crème fraîche. Serves 8.

Beet "hummus" with sautéed beet tops

I like my food to be as colorfully diverse as possible (plus that's a good way of getting all the nutrients our bodies need). Beet "hummus" is a beautiful vibrant magenta and looks almost too good to eat. Serves 6 to 8 as a snack with bread and crudités, or as part of a mixed meze.

1 quantity Boiled beets, still warm
Juice of ¼ lemon
4 Tbsp live natural yogurt
3 Tbsp extra virgin olive oil, plus more for the beet tops (if using)
1 garlic clove, crushed
1 tsp cumin seeds, toasted and crushed (see page 163)

For the beet tops (optional)
Beet tops, stalks finely chopped, leaves washed thoroughly and shredded
1 tsp cumin seeds

Quarter the warm beets and put them in a blender. Add the lemon juice, yogurt, extra virgin oil, garlic, and cumin, then blend to a smooth purée and let cool.

If you have the beet tops, sauté them in a little more olive oil 2 minutes, then add the cumin seeds. Dress the beet purée with the greens and serve with bread or raw vegetable crudités.

STORAGE Both the boiled beets and the "hummus" will keep well in sealed containers in the refrigerator 4 days. Make sure the containers are nonporous (ceramic is good), or they will stain. Return both to room temperature before serving.

COOK NATURAL Look for root veggies that still have their leaves on. The leaves perish more quickly than the root, therefore are a good indication of their freshness, and some are also good to eat. Beet tops and stalks are delicious, as are turnip greens, which are cooked into a pasta sauce in Italy. Radish tops are good, too, especially in soup (see page 50). You can also eat zucchini and squash leaves and stems, although they are harder to get hold of unless you grow your own. Try cooking them with some garlic, ginger, and coconut milk. And you can cook any of these less commonly used greens in the same way as you would winter greens (see pages 150 to 155 for more recipes).

Roast beets with garlic

I love the sweet caramelized flavors of roast beets, sticky in the pan, best eaten with plenty of garlic roasted in its skin, all the while knowing that you are filling your body with nutritious goodness. Serves 4 to 5 as a side dish.

1⅛ lb [500 g] beets, splash of light olive oil, 1 bulb of garlic separated into cloves, a few sprigs flat-leaf parsley

Preheat the oven to 350°F [180°C]. Remove the leaves of the beets. (If they are fresh, wilt them in a skillet with light olive oil and serve as greens alongside the roast beets.) Wash the beets and cut into wedges about ¾ to 1 in [2 to 3 cm] at their thickest. Toss in olive oil, salt, and pepper, place on a baking sheet with space for them to breathe, cover with foil, and put in the oven. After 30 minutes, remove the foil to allow them to take on a little color and add the garlic. After another 20 minutes or so the beet should be soft and slightly caramelized. Roughly chop the parsley leaves and finely chop the stalks and mix with the beet to serve.

MORE ROAST BEET . . . AND LEFTOVERS
With blue cheese, walnuts and rocket. Mix crumbled blue cheese into 1 quantity Roast beet with garlic and add crushed walnuts and a few leaves of rocket. Serves 2 as a salad.

With soy seeds and crispy seaweed. Toast a few tablespoons of mixed seeds in a pan with some soy sauce until they become sticky. Sprinkle over 1 quantity Roast beet with garlic along with a little crushed nori seaweed. Serves 4 to 5 as a side dish, good with Asian-inspired food.

Roast beets, pak choi, labneh, and cumin

I love eating beets with cumin and yogurt, so created this recipe to combine those flavors in a salad. This is fabulous as part of a meze, or served simply with a green salad. It's really easy to make your own labneh: place 1⅛ lb [500 g] thick full-fat live natural yogurt in a piece of muslin or a dish towel. Tie a knot to seal the cloth and suspend in a sieve over a bowl, or hang from the kitchen tap, 4 or 5 hours, or overnight, to let the whey drain away. This will yield a generous 7 oz [200 g]; enough for the recipe below. Serves 4.

1 quantity Roast beets with garlic
2 pak choi, or the beet tops if you have them, trimmed and cut into rough pieces
Glug of light olive oil
1 garlic clove, sliced
Finely grated zest and juice of 1 unwaxed lemon
7 oz [200 g] labneh (see recipe introduction) or 7 oz [200 g] thick full-fat live natural yogurt
Extra virgin olive oil, to taste
Pinch or two cumin seeds, toasted and crushed (see page 163), or to taste, plus more to serve
1 Tbsp toasted sesame seeds

Sear the pak choi or beet tops in the light olive oil in a wok or skillet just 1 minute, then add the garlic, a squeeze of lemon juice, and a little seasoning. Remove from the heat.

Season the labneh or yogurt with another squeeze of lemon, 1 tsp of the lemon zest, the extra virgin oil, cumin, and salt and pepper, adjusting the levels of lemon juice, oil, and cumin to taste.

Combine the roast beet and pak choi or beet tops, add the remaining lemon zest, and adjust the seasoning. Spoon on to a platter. Place spoonfuls of the labneh or yogurt among the veg and sprinkle the sesame seeds and more cumin seeds over the top.

STORAGE The roast beets will keep 4 days in a sealed container in the refrigerator. The salad is best served fresh, but will keep 3 days in a sealed container in the refrigerator. Return both to room temperature to serve.

Candied beets

Eat these as candies, or use them to decorate cakes. Makes about 16 slices, or as many as you can get from your beet!

1 medium beet (about 7 oz [200 g]), ¾ cup [150 g] rapadura or raw cane sugar

Wash the beet and peel it if the skin is very rough, then cut into slices as thinly as you can. Boil the sugar with 7 Tbsp [100 ml] water, stirring until the sugar has dissolved. Add the beet slices and simmer 10 minutes until sweet and soft, while preheating the oven to 340°F [170°C]. Lay the slices on baking parchment on a baking sheet, keeping the syrup to use as a sauce. Bake 10 to 15 minutes to caramelize the slices further, but be careful not to overcook them, or they will turn bubbly and burned, tasting of nothing. Let cool.

MORE CANDIED BEET . . . AND LEFTOVERS
Chocolate spread. In the unlikely situation you have leftover Chocolate pots, they make an amazingly decadent topping for toast at breakfast.

With goat's cheese. Top Candied beet slices with soft goat's cheese and serve as a canapé, or just serve the slices with a cheese board.

Chocolate pots

This is an intensely rich dessert, so the smallest pot is all you need. The candied beet pieces make nice chewy morsels. Makes 6 to 8 small pots.

1 quantity Candied beets, with syrup
7 oz [200 g] dark chocolate (70 percent cocoa solids), broken into small pieces
7 Tbsp [100 ml] Candied beet syrup, plus more to serve
⅞ cup [220 ml] heavy cream, plus more to serve

Put 6 to 8 beet slices aside to decorate the pots and chop the rest into small pieces.

Melt the chocolate in a bowl over a pan of hot (but not boiling) water. Chocolate melts at body temperature, so doesn't need excessive heat to melt it. Stir gently. When melted, remove from the heat.

Slowly stir in the beet syrup, then the cream, until the mixture is smooth.

Add the chopped beets and pour into 6 to 8 small pots. Serve each with a spoon of whipped cream, top with one of the reserved slices of candied beets, and add a drizzle of beet syrup.

STORAGE Candied beets will keep 1 month in a sealed container in the refrigerator. Chocolate pots will keep 4 days in the refrigerator, but return them to room temperature to serve.

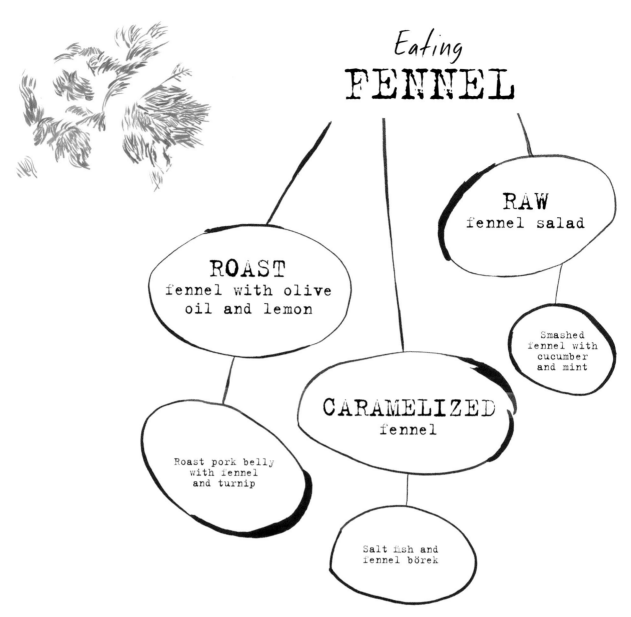

Eating
FENNEL

RAW
fennel salad

ROAST
fennel with olive
oil and lemon

Smashed
fennel with
cucumber
and mint

CARAMELIZED
fennel

Roast pork belly
with fennel
and turnip

Salt fish and
fennel börek

June to October A bulb of fennel eaten raw is the most crisp, refreshing vegetable, perfect to awaken your palate on a summer's day. It also serves as a nice fresh complement to the heavier roots and other winter vegetables that overlap with its season during mid to late fall. And, as the fall nights draw in, fennel, still thriving in the fields, can be a rich and sweet comfort when roasted, caramelized, or grilled.

When I grow my own fennel, I like to allow some to go to seed before harvesting, as you can dry the large fronds and flowers and use them in cooking during the winter. Rub the dried seeds into pork belly before a fierce scorch in the oven to produce the best crackling you've ever had (see page 104). Or make a foil parcel of fish and dried fennel fronds to highlight the herb's aniseedy aromatic oils.

When you get home from the market with your fennel bulbs, remove the fresh, frondy green fennel tops and store them in a cup of water in the refrigerator. Finely chop them and use as a herb to season fish and vegetable dishes. Store the fennel bulb separately, in a plastic bag or tub in the refrigerator. When you prepare the bulb, the outer layer can be a bit tough. Don't throw it away or compost it; instead pull it off and finely slice it before slicing the rest of the bulb as the recipe demands, to get the most out of this versatile gem.

Caramelized fennel

A fine delicacy, caramelized fennel is naturally sweet and full of flavor. It will go well with anything, but I like it best alongside a piece of fish. Serves 4 as a side dish.

2 fennel bulbs (about 1⅛ lb [500 g]), 3 garlic cloves, good glug of light olive oil

Preheat the oven to 400°F [200°C]. Remove the frondy tops and the stalks from the fennel and set aside. Cut the root off if it is brown, then cut the bulb in half from the root to the tip and cut each half into thin slices. Finely shred the stalks and the leafy tops. Put the fennel into a deep baking sheet and mix with the whole garlic cloves, the light olive oil, and a pinch of salt and pepper. Cover with foil and put into the oven 30 minutes. Remove the foil, stir, then return to the oven, reducing the temperature as you do so to 350°F [180°C]. Cook a further 30 minutes, stirring again halfway through. When the fennel is soft, sticky, and sweet, it is ready to serve.

MORE CARAMELIZED FENNEL . . . AND LEFTOVERS
Fennel pissaladière. Preheat the oven to 350°F [180°C]. Make 1 quantity Rough puff pastry (see page 82) and roll it out to ¼ in [5 mm] thick. Place it on a baking sheet. Spread a ⅜ in [1 cm] thick layer of Caramelized fennel on top. Lay as many anchovies as you dare over it, in lines. Bake in the oven 25 minutes, or until the pastry is cooked through and the top golden brown. Serves 4 as a light lunch with salad or 6 to 8 as a snack.

Caramelized fennel and olive bruschetta. Pit 4 Tbsp black olives, then finely chop them. Grill 4 pieces of your favorite bread. Rub each toast with a garlic clove, then spread a spoon of chopped olives on each. Top with a pile of Caramelized fennel. Makes 4.

Salt fish and fennel börek

Salt fish goes so well with fennel. Both are rich and strong-tasting, but the flavors stand up to each other. This isn't a traditional börek, but just about fits the criteria as it is made with filo pastry. You will need to salt the fish for 6 hours, so work that time into your preparations. Makes 2.

1 quantity Caramelized fennel, with no added salt
7 oz [200 g] fillets of white fish, such as pollack or dab
Plenty of coarse sea salt
Juice of ½ lemon
1 tsp coriander seeds, roughly crushed
4 sprigs of parsley, stalks finely chopped, leaves roughly chopped
2 sheets of filo or yufka pastry, or 1 quantity Olive oil pastry (see page 155)
Light olive oil
1 Tbsp sesame seeds

Place the fish in a nonmetallic shallow dish and sprinkle sea salt liberally over the top until it's covered. Place in the refrigerator and leave 6 hours. (If you have to use fine salt, leave just 3 hours.) Wash off the salt and pat the fish dry. Taste a small piece. If it's salty but tasty, it is fine to use. If it's inedibly salty, soak the fish in water 30 minutes. Taste and repeat if it is still too salty. When ready, pat dry with paper towels.

Preheat the oven to 350°F [180°C]. Shred the fish into small bite-size pieces. Mix it with the fennel, lemon juice, coriander seeds, and parsley.

Find an ovenproof dish that is about 8 in [20 cm] wide. If using filo or yufka, lay a sheet into the dish, overhanging the edges. Brush or drizzle with light olive oil, then fill with half the salt fish mixture. Fold the pastry over the top, brush with oil, then lay another sheet of filo over and brush it, too, with oil. Fill with the rest of the salt fish and fold the pastry over the top. If using olive oil pastry, roll it out until it is ¼ in [5 mm] thick. Lay the pastry in the ovenproof dish and fill with all the salt fish mixture. Fold the pastry over the top. Finish with a brush of oil and the sesame seeds. Put in the oven 30 minutes until hot and a dark golden brown.

STORAGE Both the fennel and the börek will keep 4 days in sealed containers in the refrigerator. Reheat both in an oven preheated to 350°F [180°C], in covered ovenproof dishes, until hot right through.

COOK NATURAL We are rarely if ever provided with the information about where store-bought salt fish came from or how it was caught. I like to make my own, so that I know. It tastes nicer, too. Look for line-caught fish and check the sustainability of the species at the time of buying. Other fish also salt well, so experiment with what is freshest on the day.

Raw fennel salad

Fennel is so delicious raw: fresh, crisp and full of flavor, crunchy like celery, but with an added sweetness. Use it for dunking in dips, or serve it with roasted or grilled fish or as part of a vegetable meze. Serves 3 to 4 as a side salad.

1 large fennel bulb (about 12¼ oz [350 g]), juice of ¼ lemon

Trim the root from the fennel bulb and remove any frondy tops, reserving them. Slice the bulb in half from top to tail, then cut each half into thin slices as you would an onion. Season with salt, pepper, and a squeeze of lemon juice, sprinkling on the reserved fronds to add sparkle.

MORE RAW FENNEL . . . AND LEFTOVERS
Fennel gin cooler. Take a glass of ice and add 5 tsp gin. Follow with 2 tsp elderflower cordial. Add a piece of cucumber, the reserved cucumber seeds from the Smashed fennel with cucumber and mint, and a slice of Raw fennel salad. Top with sparkling water, stir, and serve. Makes 1.

A fish parcel. Preheat the oven to 375°F [190°C]. Choose your favorite whole fish, scaled and gutted—any will do—and place it in the middle of a large piece of foil on a bed of Raw fennel salad. Fold up the foil around the fish and scrunch it to create a seal. Bake in the oven 15 to 30 minutes, depending on the size of the fish. Take a little peek to check it is cooked through; it should be opaque next to the spine. Serves 1 to 4, depending on the size of the fish.

Smashed fennel with cucumber and mint

This recipe is made using a rather strange method: the cucumber and fennel are smashed in a plastic bag to bruise the salad, tenderizing the vegetables and drawing out their juices. Serves 4.

7 oz [200 g] <u>Raw</u> fennel salad
7 oz [200 g] cucumber
12 mint leaves
½ cup [50 g] walnuts, crushed (optional)
½ cup [50 g] dates, roughly chopped (optional)
Drizzle of extra virgin olive oil
Juice of ½ lemon

Cut the cucumber in half lengthwise. Remove the seeds with a spoon (keep them for Fennel gin cooler, see below left). Slice the cucumber thinly. Put it in a clean plastic bag with the fennel. Tear the mint leaves and add them to the bag.

Here comes the fun part. Seal the bag at the top and slam it on the table 6 or 7 times to bruise the fennel and cucumber and let out their natural juices. Be careful the bag doesn't split; don't be too athletic!

Leave the salad in a bowl 15 minutes for the flavors to combine. Stir in the nuts and dates (if using). Taste and adjust the seasoning, then dress with extra virgin oil and lemon juice.

<u>STORAGE</u> Both salads keep 3 days in a sealed container in the refrigerator, but this is best without the mint.

Roast fennel with olive oil and lemon

Serve hot with fish or meat, or on a bruschetta with some tapenade. Serves 4 as a side dish.

2 fennel bulbs (about 1⅛ lb [500 g]), drizzle of light olive oil, lemon juice

Preheat the oven to 350°F [180°C]. If the fennel has any fronds, cut them off and reserve. Trim the root off if it is browned, then cut the fennel bulbs in half from top to tail. Next cut each half into 4 wedges, making sure each has a bit of root to hold the segments together. Put in a roasting tin, drizzle with light olive oil and a little salt, and squeeze over some lemon juice. Toss, then roast in the oven 35 to 45 minutes until browned in places and soft, turning halfway through. Serve sprinkled with the reserved fennel fronds.

MORE ROAST FENNEL . . . AND LEFTOVERS
Roast fennel couscous. Put 5¼ oz [150 g] wholemeal couscous in a small bowl, add a drizzle of light olive oil, and mix to coat the grains. Cover with hot but not boiling water, cover, and leave 5 minutes, then break up with a fork to separate the grains. Mix 1 quantity Roast fennel with olive oil and lemon through the couscous and serve with roast or grilled meat or fish, or halloumi cheese. Serves 4 as an accompaniment.

Roast fennel and olive salad. Mix a few olives into leftover Roast fennel with olive oil and lemon and serve cold.

Roast pork belly with fennel and turnip

Fennel and pork is a great combination. The sweet, subtle flavor of pork accepts and mimics the aniseed sweetness of the bulb. Serves 8.

1 quantity Roast fennel with olive oil and lemon, assembled but not yet cooked
2¼ lb [1 kg] thick end of pork belly, boned
1 tsp fennel seeds
6 garlic cloves
Sprig thyme
1⅛ lb [500 g] turnips, each cut into 8 wedges
Light olive oil
Lemon slices, to serve

Preheat the oven to 425°F [220°C]. Score the pork belly using your sharpest knife (I often ask my butcher to do this for me). Put it on a baking sheet large enough to hold the turnips and fennel, too. Fifteen minutes before cooking, rub a generous pinch of coarse salt and the fennel seeds into the meat and the skin, getting into any nooks and crannies as this is where most of the flavor will penetrate into the meat.

Put the pork in the oven 15 to 25 minutes, or until the crackling is bubbling and crispy, allowing it to become a little dark if necessary; it's worth it for a superior crackling. When the crackling is done, reduce the oven temperature to 340°F [170°C]. Toss the raw fennel, garlic cloves, thyme, and turnips in the oil and add to the baking sheet.

Roast a further 35 to 45 minutes. The best way to check if the pork is cooked is with a temperature probe and I'd strongly recommend buying one. Push the probe into the thickest part of the meat. When it reaches a temperature of more than 163°F [73°C], it's ready. If you don't have a probe, stick a sharp knife into the thickest part of the meat and check the juices run clear with no trace of pink. If you're really unsure, cut the meat and look inside: if it's opaque and white, it's cooked. Cover with foil and a dish towel and rest at least 15 minutes in a warm place. (I serve it just warm.)

Slice the pork and serve with the vegetables, lemon slices, and a sprinkle of fennel fronds.

STORAGE Both the pork and the fennel will keep really well in sealed containers in the refrigerator up to 4 days and are nice hot or cold. Reheat in an oven preheated to 350°F [180°C], until piping hot right through. Both are delicious in a sandwich.

Eating
SWEETCORN

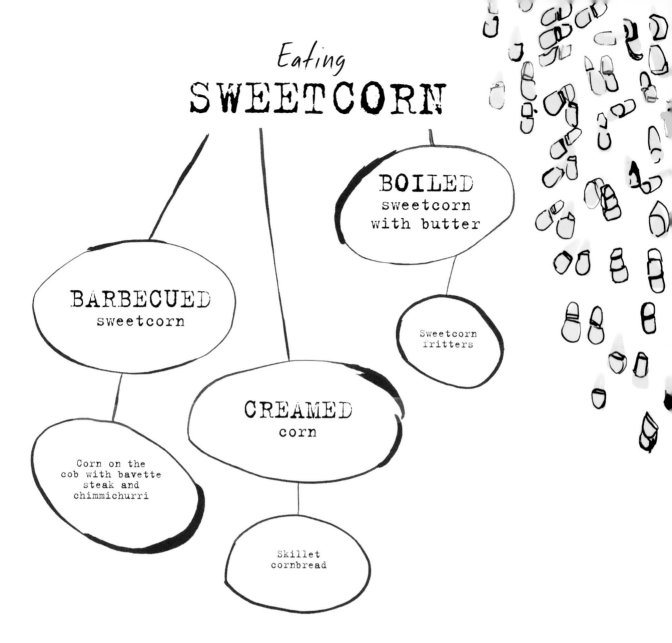

BOILED
sweetcorn
with butter

BARBECUED
sweetcorn

CREAMED
corn

Sweetcorn
fritters

Corn on the
cob with bavette
steak and
chimmichurri

Skillet
cornbread

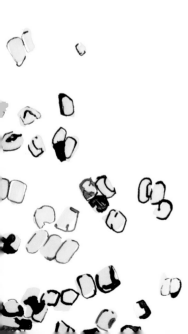

September and October We should look to Latin America for inspiration on the best way to use sweetcorn, as the Mayans, Incas, and Aztecs were cultivating it and making tortillas back in 7000 BC. In fact, some researchers claim that varieties of sweetcorn now provide about one-fifth of human global nutrition . . . the crop is certainly grown in such abundance that uses have been found for all its byproducts (including as attic insulation!).

Fresh boiled sweetcorn, smothered in salted butter, is a showstopper and perhaps the easiest way to enjoy the sweet kernels. But don't stop there, as it can be used in 101 other recipes. The golden yellow corn can be treated to my favorite end-of-summer pastime, cooking over coals. It tastes good with Chimichurri, too (see page 108). Lovely Corn fritters (see page 111) are a must on the to-do list, but make sure you use a fresh cob and not the canned stuff . . . there is no comparison. Other Latin American dishes that you must try are corn ice cream (see right), tamales (a real comfort food, corn parcels wrapped in the husk and steamed), and the little corn cakes *buñuelitos de maiz*.

Look for sweetcorn cobs in their husks and store them in the refrigerator, as they will keep for longer. Buy and eat sweetcorn as fresh as possible, to catch the cobs at their sweetest.

Creamed corn

I wouldn't touch the canned stuff but, made with fresh corn cut from the cob, this is a sumptuous dish. Serves 4 as a side dish.

2 sweetcorn cobs, 3½ Tbsp [50 ml] heavy cream, knob of butter

Stand the corn on its end, hold it firmly, and cut off the kernels with a sharp knife in long strokes. Now break them up with your hands. Next, using a soup spoon, scrape all the mushy pulp and "milk" out of the cob. Put the pulp and kernels into a heavy-based pan or skillet with the cream, butter, and 3½ Tbsp [50 ml] water. Bring to a boil, then reduce the heat and simmer gently 10 minutes, until the cream begins to thicken. Season to taste, then serve.

MORE CREAMED CORN . . . AND LEFTOVERS
Chowder. Finely chop 1 onion, 1 potato, and 1 celery stick and gently fry in light olive oil 10 minutes with 1 sprig thyme. Add 1 quantity Creamed corn and 2 cups [500 ml] milk. Bring to a boil, then reduce to a gentle simmer and cook for 15 minutes. Add 10½ oz [300 g] flaked smoked fish, or some cooked bacon lardoons, if you like. Serves 4.

Creamed corn ice cream. Add 2 cups [500 ml] heavy cream and 1¼ cups [300 ml] whole milk to 1 quantity unseasoned Creamed corn and bring to a boil. Meanwhile, whisk 8 egg yolks with ¼ cup [50 g] rapadura or raw cane sugar until it thickens. Add the hot creamed corn to the egg yolk mixture, stirring constantly, then return to the pan over very low heat. Cook a few minutes, stirring constantly, while it thickens. Strain out the corn, returning just a couple of spoons to the pudding (save the rest for reheating and eating as an extra-rich side dish). Freeze in a freezer-proof container, whisking every 2 hours until it is set. Serve in scoops as a simple dessert. Makes about 4½ cups [1 L].

Skillet cornbread

Cornbread is ultra-fast to prepare and really makes a meal complete. As I'm a real fan of spicy food, I like to add a sliced jalapeño chili. This is good with chili con carne or a stew. Serves 8 as an accompaniment.

1 quantity Creamed corn
10½ oz [300 g] coarse polenta or cornmeal
1 jalapeño chili, finely sliced (optional)
1 cup [250 ml] live natural yogurt
2 eggs, lightly beaten
2 tsp baking powder
½ tsp bicarbonate of soda
Butter, for the pan

Preheat the oven to 400°F [200°C]. Mix all the ingredients except the butter together thoroughly, adding 1 tsp salt

Butter a 9 to 10 in [22 to 25 cm] skillet or ovenproof skillet and pour in the batter. Cook in the oven 10 to 15 minutes, until the bread is golden and springy to the touch.

STORAGE Both the creamed corn and the bread will keep 3 days in sealed containers in the refrigerator. Reheat the creamed corn in a saucepan with a little milk, if needed, to loosen the texture. The cornbread is great at room temperature.

Barbecued sweetcorn

Some people barbecue sweetcorn, from raw, in the husk, but I find it just stays a little too chewy that way. Parboiling it gives you the best of both worlds, with succulent juicy kernels and a good barbecue taste. Serves 4 as a side dish.

4 sweetcorn cobs, light olive oil

Bring a large pan of salted water to a boil and remove the husks and silk from the corn, keeping some of the husks to use as serving plates. Put the sweetcorn in the boiling water, cover, and cook 8 minutes. Drain and let cool. Meanwhile, light the barbecue with plenty of coals. Wait until they are white hot, then spread them out evenly and let cool slightly. Or heat a griddle pan over high heat. Roll the sweetcorn cobs in light olive oil and season with salt. Barbecue or griddle the corn until it chars in places, then turn and cook evenly all over. The cooking time will depend on the heat of your barbecue, so judge with your eyes. Serve as it is, in the reserved husks.

MORE BARBECUED SWEETCORN . . . AND LEFTOVERS
Burrito. Excellent if you have leftover steak, Barbecued sweetcorn and chimichurri. Boil ¼ cup [50 g] brown rice per person. Cut the kernels from the cobs and slice the steak. Heat tortillas in a pan or on the barbecue, then fill with rice, steak, corn, and a good helping of chimichurri. Wrap and enjoy.

Romesco. This sauce (see page 37) is good to serve with steak and Barbecued sweetcorn.

Corn on the cob with bavette steak and chimichurri

Chimichurri is an Argentinian condiment, similar to a vinegary salsa verde but with a touch of chili. Traditionally it is served with beef, but it works really well with most things cooked on a barbecue. Serves 4 as an entree, or more as a snack.

For the corn and steak
1 quantity Barbecued sweetcorn, boiled but not yet chargrilled
1¾ lb [800 g] strip of bavette steak
Light olive oil

For the chimichurri
2½ Tbsp parsley, finely chopped
2 tsp dried oregano, or chopped fresh sprigs of oregano
2 garlic cloves, crushed
Pinch of chili flakes
8 Tbsp extra virgin olive oil
3 Tbsp red wine vinegar

Chimichurri gets better as it matures, so make it first (or, even better, the day before). Mix all the ingredients together and set aside for the flavors to mellow.

Light the barbecue following the instructions given left. Season the steak with plenty of salt and pepper and rub it well with light olive oil.

Barbecue the corn at the same time as the steak; this should give enough time to cook the steak and allow it to rest. Allow the steak to color and slightly char on one side, then turn and char again. If you like your steak rare, remove it from the heat now and allow it to rest. If you like it medium, cook a further minute each side then rest a few minutes. If you like well-done steak, I'd recommend asking your butcher to butterfly the steak into a thin slice for quick cooking.

Once rested, slice the bavette across the grain. Serve with the corn, smothering both in chimichurri.

STORAGE Chimichurri will keep in a sealed container in the refrigerator 4 days, as will both the cooked meat and the barbecued corn. Return everything to room temperature before serving, or turning into Burritos (see left).

COOK NATURAL When lighting a barbecue, make the most of it by going through the refrigerator to find any other vegetables that will be good grilled. Excellent candidates are past-their-best bell peppers or eggplants, artichokes, zucchini, fennel bulbs, and leeks. Cook them all at the same time for a chargrilled vegetable feast. Keep leftovers in the refrigerator and dress with vinaigrette for a chargrilled vegetable salad.

Boiled sweetcorn with butter

The simplest way to eat sweetcorn. Serves 2 to 4 as a side dish.

2 large sweetcorn cobs, 4 Tbsp [50 g] butter

Bring a large saucepan of salted water to a rolling boil. Remove the husks and silk from the corn, add to the pan, and cover. Boil 10 to 12 minutes, then drain and smear with butter.

MORE BOILED SWEETCORN . . . AND LEFTOVERS
Chutney. Cut the kernels from 1 quantity Boiled sweetcorn, without butter. Finely chop 1 small onion and 1 chili and put them in a saucepan with ⅜ cup [80 g] rapadura or raw cane sugar, 1 tsp salt, and 7 Tbsp [100 ml] cider vinegar. Bring to a boil, then reduce the heat and simmer 10 minutes. Mix 1 Tbsp spelt or wholemeal flour with a dash of water to make a paste. Stir the flour paste and sweetcorn into the vinegar mixture and boil a further 5 minutes, until thickened. Pour into a sterilized jar (see page 52) and keep in the refrigerator 2 to 3 weeks. This is particularly nice served with burgers. Makes about one 1⅛ lb [500 g] jar.

Bean and cilantro salad. Cut the kernels from 1 quantity Boiled sweetcorn, without butter. Drain and rinse a 14 oz [400 g] can of kidney beans and mix with the kernels. Add three sprigs cilantro, chopped, a dash of extra virgin oil and red wine vinegar, and seasoning. Serves 4 as a side salad.

Sweetcorn fritters

These are remarkably good, a great snack or appetizer. I like mine with chili sauce . . . but it does mask the sweetness of the corn. Serves 4.

1 quantity Boiled sweetcorn, without butter
1¼ cups [150 g] spelt or wholemeal flour
1 egg, lightly beaten
½ tsp baking powder
4 scallions, finely chopped
6 sprigs cilantro, stalks finely chopped, leaves
  roughly chopped
Flavorless vegetable oil, to shallow-fry
Chili sauce or sour cream, to serve

Cut the kernels from the sweetcorn cobs. Mix the flour, egg, and baking powder, gradually adding 7 Tbsp [100 ml] water to make a thick batter, then season well with salt and pepper. Add the scallions, cilantro, and sweetcorn to the batter and mix.

Heat a heavy-based skillet or skillet over medium heat with a glug of the oil. Fry spoonfuls of the fritters, flattening them a little with the back of the spoon. When they are golden brown, flip them over and fry on the other side. Keep warm while you cook the rest. Serve with chili sauce or sour cream.

STORAGE The fritters will keep 3 days in a sealed container in the refrigerator. Reheat in an oven preheated to 350°F [180°C] 12 minutes, or until hot right through. A boiled sweetcorn is best eaten immediately, but can be cut from the cob and reheated in a saucepan with a little butter.

Eating
APPLES

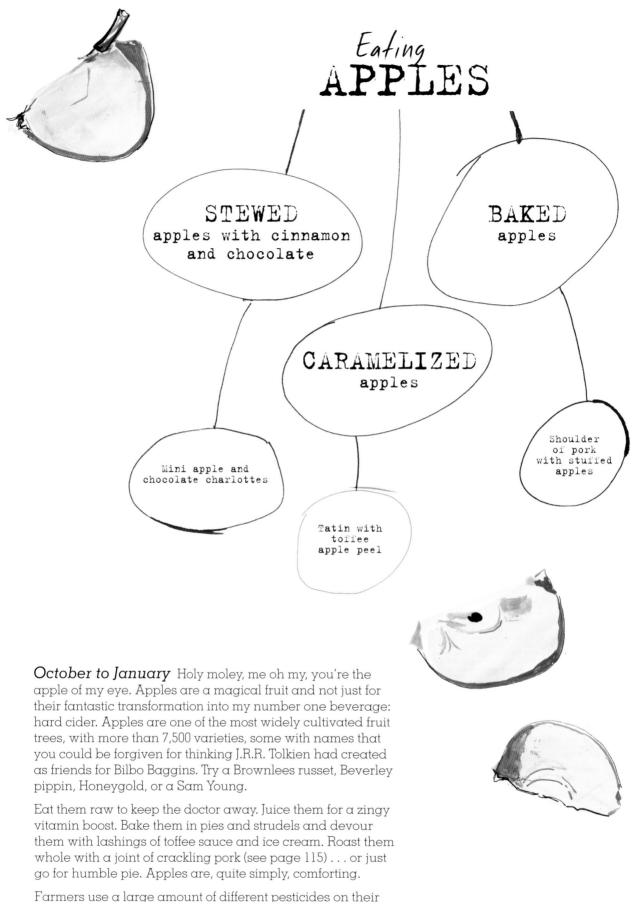

STEWED
apples with cinnamon
and chocolate

BAKED
apples

CARAMELIZED
apples

Mini apple and
chocolate charlottes

Tatin with
toffee
apple peel

Shoulder
of pork
with stuffed
apples

October to January Holy moley, me oh my, you're the apple of my eye. Apples are a magical fruit and not just for their fantastic transformation into my number one beverage: hard cider. Apples are one of the most widely cultivated fruit trees, with more than 7,500 varieties, some with names that you could be forgiven for thinking J.R.R. Tolkien had created as friends for Bilbo Baggins. Try a Brownlees russet, Beverley pippin, Honeygold, or a Sam Young.

Eat them raw to keep the doctor away. Juice them for a zingy vitamin boost. Bake them in pies and strudels and devour them with lashings of toffee sauce and ice cream. Roast them whole with a joint of crackling pork (see page 115) . . . or just go for humble pie. Apples are, quite simply, comforting.

Farmers use a large amount of different pesticides on their orchards to protect apple crops from fungus and insect threats. This leaves high levels of pesticide residues on the fruit itself so, whenever possible, buy organic.

Stewed apples with cinnamon and chocolate

If you have any apples that need using up fast, this is a great recipe for them. Keep these in the refrigerator for breakfast, or use as a simple dessert. Try to use a mixture of cooking apples, which will cook down into a purée, and tart eating apples such as Cox's Orange Pippin, which will stay in chunks. Serves 4.

1⅛ lb [500 g] apples, ½ cup [100 g] light muscovado sugar, juice of ½ lemon, grating of nutmeg, pinch of ground cinnamon, 2 oz [60 g] dark chocolate

Cut the apples into ¾ to 1 in [2 to 3 cm] cubes, removing the peels and cores as you go (freeze the cores, see bottom right). Put the apple flesh in a deep saucepan with all the other ingredients except the chocolate. Place over medium heat and bring to a boil, then reduce the heat to a simmer and cover. Simmer 8 to 10 minutes, or until they are soft but still have some shape. Break the chocolate into small pieces and stir it into the apples, then remove from the heat. Serve immediately, or leave for a few minutes, stirring a little more, depending on whether you want chunks of chocolate or a smooth chocolatey sauce.

MORE STEWED APPLES . . . AND LEFTOVERS
Crème brûlée. Place a little leftover Stewed apples with cinnamon and chocolate at the bottom of 4 ramekins. Top with Crème brûlée pudding (see page 21; follow the instructions there for baking). Makes 4.

With granola. Spoon leftover Stewed apples with cinnamon and chocolate on your breakfast Granola (see page 21).

Mini apple and chocolate charlottes

A very tempting little dessert. The chocolate soaks into the bread and becomes a little caramelized and crunchy. You will need a deep muffin pan. Makes 6 to 8.

1 quantity Stewed apples with cinnamon and chocolate
4½ Tbsp [60 g] butter, softened
⅜ cup [50 g] light muscovado sugar
6 to 7 thin slices of sourdough or wholemeal bread, crusts removed

Preheat the oven to 400°F [200°C]. Mix the butter and sugar together and spread it on both sides of the slices of bread. Cut the bread to line the *sides only* of 6 to 8 muffin molds, sticking it on with the butter, overlapping it slightly, and pressing together so the sides are sealed. Leave the bottoms of the molds open. Cut out "tops" (which when turned out will become bottoms) with the leftover bread.

Fill each mold tightly with apples, then add the buttered bread "tops" and press down firmly to seal with the bread sides. Bake in the hot oven about 20 minutes, until the charlottes bubble and become a little crispy on top.

Be patient and let it cool a bit. Run a knife around the edges and carefully prize each charlotte out of its mold with a spoon. If one falls apart, gently encourage it back together. The exposed apple at the top should look caramelized and inviting. Serve warm or cold with crème fraîche or yogurt.

STORAGE The stewed apples will keep 4 days in a sealed container in the refrigerator. The charlottes are best eaten immediately, but will keep in an airtight container 3 days. Reheat them gently in a warm oven to crisp up once more before serving.

COOK NATURAL Apple peelings should be eaten and not thrown away or composted, for they contain most of the nutrients. Leave them on when cooking if you can, or keep the peelings with the cores in the freezer until you have at least 2 lb [1 kg], to make a pectin-rich liquid to add to jams and jellies. Just put them in a pot, not quite covered with water, bring to a boil, and simmer 45 minutes. Allow to strain overnight through a jelly bag—or a dish towel or piece of muslin—into a bowl. Squeeze every last bit of the liquid out of the cloth. Use the liquid to set low-pectin fruit jam, such as plum, by adding an equal quantity to the fruit or juice, then following the jam recipe. Using this liquid pectin also allows you to make your preserve with raw cane sugar instead of highly processed and refined white sugar.

Baked apples

These make a great dessert. I like to use a tart eating apple such as a Cox's Orange Pippin or Braeburn, something not too big, so that you can serve an apple to each person. Serves 4.

4 apples, ¼ cup [40 g] black or golden raisins, 4 tsp rapadura or raw cane sugar, 1½ Tbsp butter, pinch of ground cinnamon

Preheat the oven to 350°F [180°C]. Remove the apple cores with a corer or knife (keep them in the freezer, see page 113). Score the apples around their equators to stop them exploding in the oven (we didn't for the photo, as it can be quite fun!). Make the stuffing by mashing together the raisins with the sugar, butter, and cinnamon until they are thoroughly mixed. Use this mixture to stuff the holes left in the apples by their cores. Place on a baking sheet and bake 25 to 30 minutes. When the apples are soft to the touch, they are ready. Be careful not to overcook them. Serve hot, with ice cream.

MORE BAKED APPLES . . . AND LEFTOVERS
Baked apple sauce. For a delicious and intensely fruity sauce for pork, blend leftover Baked apples, or chop by hand.

Apple, black pudding, and pork pie. If you have any leftovers of the pork and black pudding apples, then make a delicious pie filling. Preheat the oven to 350°F [180°C]. Chop the pork and apples into bite-size pieces, then use them to fill a suitably sized pie dish and top with Rough puff or Shortcrust pastry (see pages 82 and 28). Bake 30 minutes.

Shoulder of pork with stuffed apples

A dish to warm you up on a cold day. Black pudding is feared by many, but in reality it's a nice sweet sausage, made from mostly oatmeal. Serves 4.

For the apples
1 quantity Baked apples, stuffing mixed, but apples not yet stuffed or cooked
2 oz [60 g] black pudding (save the rest for breakfast)

For the roast pork
2¼ lb [1 kg] boned and rolled shoulder of pork
3½ Tbsp [50 ml] brandy or white wine

Preheat the oven to 400°F [200°C]. Mash the black pudding into the apple stuffing mixture, then stuff the apples, as for the Baked apples recipe (see left). Set aside.

Season the pork with salt and pepper and put in a roasting tray in the oven. After 20 minutes, reduce the oven temperature to 340°F [170°C]. Leave for 1½ hours. Remove from the oven and baste, spooning the juices over the meat. Add the stuffed apples to the tray and return to the oven 25 to 30 minutes; they should be soft and colored.

Place the apples and pork on a warmed serving plate. Skim any excess fat from the roasting tray with a spoon, then put it over medium heat. Add the brandy or wine and bring to a boil. (The brandy might catch fire for a second, so stand back.) Scrape the base of the roasting tray, stirring back in all the sticky juices from the apples and pork.

Pour the rich juices over the meat and apples and serve with roast potatoes and a green salad.

STORAGE The pork and apples will keep well in sealed containers in the refrigerator 4 days. Reheat both in an oven preheated to 350°F [180°C] until piping hot, before serving.

Caramelized apples

These are delicious served with yogurt or crème fraîche for breakfast or pudding. Serves 6 to 8.

2 lb [900 g] tart eating apples (such as Cox's Orange Pippin or Braeburn), ¾ cup [150 g] rapadura or raw cane sugar

Peel the apples (reserve the peelings, see right to make toffee apple peel, or page 113 to make a liquid pectin for jam). Cut the apples in half and remove the cores with a knife (freeze them, see page 113). Take a heavy-based ovenproof skillet 8 to 10 in [20 to 25 cm] in diameter, place it over medium heat, and sprinkle the sugar evenly over the base. Now fill the pan with the apples, cut-sides down, tightly packed together. Allow to boil and bubble slowly 20 minutes without moving the apples, then turn the apples so they are all rounded-side down. Cook a further 15 minutes until the juices mostly evaporate, leaving a thin caramel sauce.

MORE CARAMELIZED APPLES . . . AND LEFTOVERS
Off-cut pastry biscuits. I always cook pastry off-cuts with spices and salt or sugar, as they make great cookies. Preheat the oven to 400°F [200°C]. Lay the off-cuts on a baking sheet and sprinkle with muscovado sugar and ground cinnamon, then bake 15 minutes until golden.

Frangipane. Follow the frangipane recipe on page 82 but replace the apricots with 1 quantity Caramelized apples. Makes about 12 portions.

Tatin with toffee apple peel

This is a classic dish and I've kept it that way, with the rather fabulous addition of toffee apple peelings. Serves 6 to 8.

1 quantity Caramelized apples, in their ovenproof pan, plus their peelings, separately
1 quantity Rough puff pastry (see page 82)
All-purpose flour, to dust
¾ cup [150 g] rapadura or raw cane sugar

Preheat the oven to 400°F [200°C]. Roll out the pastry on a lightly floured work surface to about ¼ in [5 mm] thick, then lay it over the top of the already cooked and caramelized apples in their pan and tuck it down between the apples and the pan edge. Freeze the excess pastry for future use (or see below left, or there are lots of other ideas for using pastry leftovers in the book; take a look around).

Put the tatin in the oven and bake 20 to 25 minutes, until the pastry is golden brown and looks cooked through. Allow to rest 30 minutes or more, so it has a chance to cool down and set.

Meanwhile, make the toffee apple peelings. Place a sheet of baking parchment over a rolling pin. Melt the sugar in a small skillet over low heat. As soon as it dissolves, drop in the peelings 2 at a time, coat with sugar on each side, then lay over the parchment and let cool. If you have any sugar left, drizzle lines of it, too, over the parchment and leave to set.

Serve the tatin with yogurt, to combat the sweetness of the apples, with the toffee apple peel and any caramel strands you made arranged on top.

STORAGE Both the tatin and the caramelized apples will keep well in sealed containers in the refrigerator 3 days. Return to room temperature to serve.

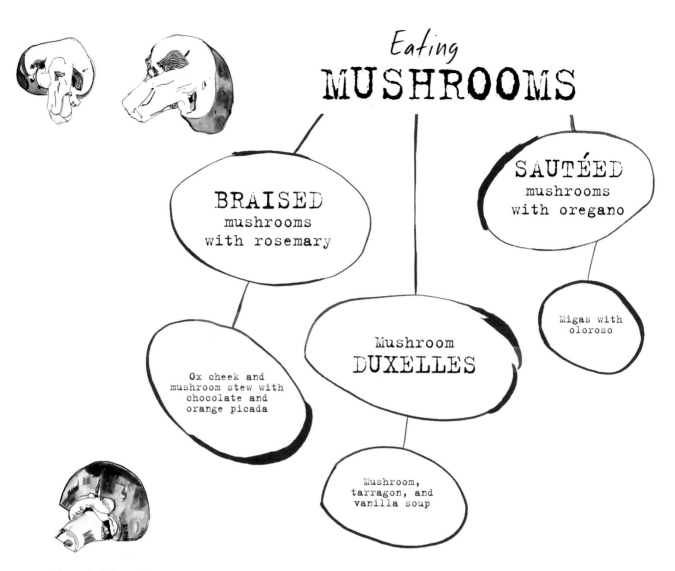

Eating
MUSHROOMS

BRAISED
mushrooms
with rosemary

SAUTÉED
mushrooms
with oregano

Mushroom
DUXELLES

Ox cheek and
mushroom stew with
chocolate and
orange picada

Migas with
oloroso

Mushroom,
tarragon, and
vanilla soup

Available all year round, but wild main crop September to November
Earthy, savory, rich—even mystical—mushrooms bring a touch of alchemy to the kitchen.
Their pungent aromas work their umami magic stirred into our domestic cauldron.
Umami is described as the fifth taste, with the same characteristics as monosodium
glutamate but without the stigma: meaty, rounded, and satisfying.

Think of the deeply savory mushroom possibilities: sautéed in a skillet with butter on
sourdough toast with freshly cracked pepper; a meaty grilled portobello with melted blue
cheese sandwiched in a bun for lunch; or red wine-braised in a dark casserole for dinner
(see page 121). Mushrooms are full of flavor.

Fortunately, commercially grown varieties of mushrooms use very few pesticides. The
main cultivated mushrooms that we see on our shelves—labeled "button," "chestnut,"
and "portobello"—are all the same variety at different stages of growth. Shiitake and
oyster mushrooms are also now widely grown in this country. Shiitake mushrooms are
a true superfood, full of antioxidants, iron, and lentinan, a compound believed to be a
natural immunity booster.

Buy squeaky-fresh, dry mushrooms without the damp spots that cause them to rot.
Keep mushrooms fresh by removing them from plastic packaging and storing in
a glass container or a paper bag in the refrigerator, with plenty of space for them to
breathe. Never wash mushrooms, as they soak up water and become soggy. Instead,
brush off dirt if necessary.

Mushroom stalks are delicious and can be cooked and eaten with the caps. If they
are particularly woody, use them instead to add their delicious musky woodland
fragrance to stocks and soup.

Sautéed mushrooms with oregano

Serve on toast with a poached egg. Serves 4 as a side dish.

14 oz [400 g] chestnut mushrooms, 1 shallot, 1½ Tbsp butter, glug of light olive oil, 2 garlic cloves, 2 sprigs oregano

Cut the mushrooms into irregular ¾ to 1 in [2 to 3 cm] chunks and roughly chop the shallot. Fry both in the butter in a heavy-based pan over medium heat with the light olive oil. Stir, and add more oil if necessary. Cook about 10 minutes, until dark and rich. Finely slice the garlic and add it to the pan with the oregano. Sauté a further 2 minutes to allow the garlic to cook but not burn, and season lightly to serve.

MORE SAUTÉED MUSHROOMS . . . AND LEFTOVERS
Barley risotto. Make a vegetable stock (see page 13), then strain it. Add 10½ oz [300 g] barley to 1 quantity Sautéed mushrooms with oregano, cover with plenty of the hot stock, and leave to simmer, adding more stock when needed, 25 to 30 minutes. (Taste to check the texture of the barley, so you know when it is perfectly cooked.) Add herbs and/or grated cheese to serve, if you like. Serves 4.

Banh mi. Leftover Sautéed mushrooms with oregano are great used to fill a Banh mi (see page 40). Mix 1 tsp raw honey with 1 tsp brown miso and 2 Tbsp water and stir to make a sauce. Stuff a baguette with the mushrooms and dress with the miso dressing. Finish with a sprinkle of crushed walnuts. Serves 4 as a light lunch.

Migas with oloroso

Migas are a Spanish dish of flavored croutons that are used as an accompaniment to an entree. It is another good way to use up stale bread, as it soaks up all the delicious flavors of the other ingredients. Serves 4 as a side dish.

1 quantity Sautéed mushrooms with oregano
1 crust of sourdough or other good, robust bread
Glug of light olive oil
2 Tbsp oloroso sherry or white wine

Rip or cut the bread into irregular ¾ to 1 in [2 to 3 cm] pieces. Soak the pieces in a bowl of water until they become soft. If fresh, this will take a few seconds; if hard and stale, a couple of minutes. Squeeze out the water and lay the pieces on a plate.

Heat a sauté pan with the light olive oil. Add the bread; be careful as it might spit. Fry until it has a nice light brown color on all sides, then add the mushrooms and allow them to reheat. Add the oloroso or wine and turn the mushrooms in the sauce.

Boil 2 minutes to allow the alcohol to burn off, then season and serve.

STORAGE Both the sautéed mushrooms and the migas will keep well in sealed containers in the refrigerator 3 days. Reheat both in a sauté pan, with a splash more oil if needed, until hot.

Braised mushrooms with rosemary

These are meaty and satisfying. Serves 4 as a side dish.

1 onion, 1 carrot, 3 garlic cloves, 4 Tbsp [50 g] butter, 14 oz [400 g] portobello or field mushrooms, 2 sprigs rosemary

Thinly slice the onion, slice the carrot into rounds, and roughly chop the garlic. Heat a heavy-based flameproof casserole dish over medium heat, add the butter and then the onion, carrot, and garlic. Sauté 15 minutes until soft and browned. Meanwhile, preheat the oven to 350°F [180°C]. Cut the mushrooms into large chunks, then add to the onions with the rosemary. Sauté 5 minutes, until they take on a little color. Add ⅝ cup [150 ml] water, bring to a boil, and scrape any sticky bits from the base of the pan. Taste, season, cover, and put in the oven 15 minutes. Eat hot with rice and veggies.

MORE BRAISED MUSHROOMS . . . AND LEFTOVERS
Little pies. If you have any leftovers of either Braised mushrooms with rosemary or the beef casserole, they make a great filling for pies. Preheat the oven to 350°F [180°C]. Line the molds of a muffin pan with Rough puff or Shortcrust pastry (see pages 82 and 28), fill each one with the filling, then top with more pastry. Bake 25 to 30 minutes.

Pasta. Any leftovers of the casserole make a delicious pasta sauce; it goes especially well with spelt tagliatelle or gigli pasta shapes. Just reheat the sauce, cutting up any large pieces of meat or mushrooms, then mix into the hot al dente pasta with a spoonful or two of the pasta cooking water.

Ox cheek and mushroom stew with chocolate and orange picada

Picada is a traditional Spanish seasoning that is added to a stew near the end of cooking to thicken it and give flavor. This is a particularly aromatic and rich version. Serves 4.

1 quantity Braised mushrooms with rosemary
14 oz [400 g] ox cheek or stewing steak, cut into pieces of similar size to the mushrooms
Light olive oil
1¼ cups [300 ml] red wine

For the picada
½ slice of robust bread
1 garlic clove, roughly chopped
4 to 5 walnuts
3 sprigs flat-leaf parsley, roughly chopped
2 tsp good dark chocolate, finely chopped
1 tsp finely grated orange zest

Preheat the oven to 340°F [170°C]. Season the beef with salt and pepper. In a hot skillet, using light olive oil, fry batches of the meat until they have a good brown color all over. This is where the flavor comes from, so don't take shortcuts and don't overcrowd the pan. When all the meat is browned, add the wine to the pan and bring to a boil, scraping any sticky bits from the base.

Put the meat and wine in a casserole dish with the mushrooms, cover, and cook in the oven 2 hours, stirring halfway through.

Meanwhile, make the picada. Soak the bread in water for a few seconds, then squeeze out the water and tear it up. Crush the garlic in a mortar and pestle with a little salt, then add the walnuts and parsley and smash once more. Grind in the bread, chocolate, and orange zest and add a little pepper. (If you don't have a mortar and pestle, the picada will be fine cut by hand.)

Ten minutes before the casserole is ready, pull it out of the oven and sprinkle the picada evenly over the top. Put it back in the oven for the remaining cooking time, with the lid on. Serve with polenta or mashed potatoes.

STORAGE The stew will get better with time and will keep 4 days in a sealed container in the refrigerator, as will the braised mushrooms. Reheat both gently on the stovetop in covered saucepans until hot right through, to serve.

Mushroom duxelles

Pick mushrooms with a good dark color. Duxelles is rich and full of flavor, delicious as a pâté spread on toast or in more complex dishes such as Venison Wellington (see below). Experiment with different mushrooms when you have them . . . a few ceps added go a long way. If you'd like to make it richer, add a dash of cream with the garlic. Serves 4 as a side dish.

1 onion, 1½ Tbsp butter (plus more if needed), splash of light olive oil, 14 oz [400 g] field mushrooms, 2 sprigs thyme, 4 garlic cloves

Finely chop the onion and sauté in a heavy-based pan over medium heat 5 minutes with the butter and light olive oil. Meanwhile, cut the mushrooms into ⅜ to ¾ in [1 to 2 cm] pieces and add to the pan. Pick the thyme leaves and add them, too. Reduce the heat and sauté slowly a further 15 minutes, adding more butter if the pan becomes dry. Roughly chop the garlic, add that, and cook a further 2 minutes. If there is still a lot of juice around the mushrooms, increase the heat and reduce it to a rich sauce.

MORE MUSHROOM DUXELLES . . . AND LEFTOVERS
Venison Wellington. Sear a 1½ lb [700 g] piece of venison loin until browned all over. Lay 4 slices of prosciutto next to each other to form a sheet. Spread a thin layer of cooled Mushroom duxelles over it, then lay the venison in the middle and wrap the prosciutto around it. Wrap tightly in a clean plastic bag and place in the refrigerator 10 minutes while you preheat the oven to 350°F [180°C]. Roll out 1 quantity Rough puff pastry (see page 82) into a large square big enough to wrap around the loin. Brush the edges with beaten egg and place the venison in the middle, wrapping the pastry around it. Press the edges tightly together, sealing the meat inside and brush with the remaining beaten egg. Bake in the oven 25 minutes until the pastry is a nice dark brown. Serves 4.

Pâté. Add 3½ oz [100 g] ricotta to the Mushroom duxelles and blend. Adjust the seasoning to serve. This will keep in the refrigerator 4 days. Serves 4 as an appetizer with toast.

Mushroom, tarragon, and vanilla soup

Sounds quirky, but it works. Go easy with the vanilla . . . we're looking for a just a hint poking through the earthy mushrooms. Serves 4.

1 quantity Mushroom duxelles
Drop of vanilla extract
4 tsp crème fraîche (optional)

For the quick veg stock (makes 4½ cups [1 L])
1 carrot, grated
1 onion, grated
1 celery stick, grated
The woody mushroom stalks
Green top of a leek, finely chopped (optional)
Parsley or other herb stalks (optional)
1 bay leaf
A few tarragon stalks, leaves saved for the soup

This is a fast, easy stock that you can use for any soup. Place all the ingredients in a tall pan with 5 cups [1.1 L] water. (Add whatever vegetables you have, all ingredients are optional.) Cover, bring to a boil, then reduce the heat and simmer 25 minutes.

Add most of the mushrooms and tarragon leaves to the stock. There's no need to remove the vegetables as they will bulk out the soup. Add the vanilla extract, remove the bay leaf and herb stalks, and blend everything else until smooth. Taste and adjust the seasoning, adding plenty of pepper. Serve in warmed bowls with the remaining mushrooms and tarragon leaves, with 1 tsp crème fraîche on each, if using.

STORAGE Both the duxelles and the soup will keep in sealed containers in the refrigerator 4 days. Reheat the soup to just below boiling point to serve, or reheat the duxelles until piping hot right through.

COOK NATURAL Making a quick and easy veg stock takes very little effort and is a good way to get the most out of your vegetables. Clean out your veg drawer and make a stock bursting with nutrition, or save veg peelings and tough herb stalks in the refrigerator or freezer until you have enough to make a stock such as the one above. There is no steadfast recipe needed, but I usually try to include carrot, onion, celery, and leek as a base and add to those. Use whatever veg and peelings you have available.

Raw carrots grated with seeds

This salad is super-fast to make and delicious for lunch; I especially like to eat it with falafels and hummus. No need to peel the carrots, just give them a good scrub. Substitute the sesame seeds with any other seeds, if you prefer. Serves 2 to 3 as a side salad.

7 oz [200 g] carrots, extra virgin olive oil, squeeze of lemon juice, 1 Tbsp sesame seeds

Grate the carrots coarsely, then dress with a splash of extra virgin oil, a little lemon juice, and salt and pepper. Toast the sesame seeds in a dry pan until they brown slightly. Mix and serve.

MORE RAW CARROTS . . . AND LEFTOVERS
Carrot-stuffed parathas. Replace the filling for Cauliflower-stuffed parathas (see page 164) with Raw carrots grated with seeds.

Carrot and beet cake. Preheat the oven to 350°F [180°C] and oil an 8 in [20 cm] round cake tin. In a bowl, mix ½ cup [100 g] rapadura or raw cane sugar with 2 lightly beaten eggs, 4½ Tbsp [70 ml] olive oil, ¾ cup [100 g] spelt flour, 1½ tsp baking powder, and a pinch of ground cinnamon. When combined, stir in 1 quantity Fall slaw with greens, beets, blackberries, seeds, and sprouts, without the salt and pepper. Pour the mixture into the cake tin and bake 25 to 30 minutes. Check it's cooked by touching the top to see if it is set and a little springy. Let cool in the tin. Serves 8.

Fall slaw with greens, beets, blackberries, seeds, and sprouts

This is a vibrant salad to eat in the fall, full of so many raw nutrients. Play around with different ingredients as the seasons change . . . as winter hits, substitute the blackberries for dried fruits and grate in whatever raw root veg you have, from kohlrabi to celery root. To sprout your own mung beans, cover them with plenty of water and leave to soak overnight. Next day, drain them and leave in a covered bowl or sealed glass jar. Rinse and drain twice a day. After 2 days they will have started to sprout and be edible. After 3 days they will have good-size sprouts. Put them in the refrigerator until you're ready to use them. Serves 4.

1 quantity Raw carrots grated with seeds
1¾ oz [50 g] sprouted mung beans
1 small beet (about 5¼ oz [150 g])
3 beet tops or kale leaves, shredded
2 Tbsp sunflower seeds
2 Tbsp pumpkin seeds
Juice of ½ lemon
Small bunch parsley, roughly chopped
5¼ oz [150 g] blackberries
Glug of extra virgin olive oil

Put the carrots into a large shallow dish. Grate the beet and add it to the dish, but do not mix the salad until you are ready to eat, so the colors stay separate (see photo, right).

Add all the remaining ingredients and season to taste. Toss to coat with the oil, then serve.

STORAGE The salad will keep 3 days in a sealed container in the refrigerator, but is best eaten straightaway, as are the raw carrots.

COOK NATURAL Feast with your eyes and eat the rainbow. The simplest way to ensure a varied and nutritious diet is by eating as many different-colored vegetables as you can. Colorful vegetables contain different vitamins and minerals and various antioxidants that help build a balanced and healthy diet.

Boiled carrots with caraway

Try serving carrots like this for a refreshing take on a simple staple. The caraway brings out the sweetness of the carrots. Serves 2 as a side dish.

7 oz [200 g] carrots, pinch or two of caraway seeds,
3 to 4 sprigs parsley, extra virgin olive oil

Wash the carrots and halve lengthwise from top to tail, quartering any that are really large. Put into a pan with a good pinch of salt, cover with cold water, and bring to a boil. Simmer about 5 minutes until they are still firm to the bite, but have lost their crunch. Meanwhile, toast the caraway seeds in a dry pan until they brown slightly. Drain the carrots (reserve the liquid if you need to make a stock or soup) and dress with the caraway, chopped parsley, and extra virgin oil. Serve hot or at room temperature.

MORE BOILED CARROTS . . . AND LEFTOVERS
Carrot and caraway soup. Prepare 1 quantity Boiled carrots with caraway and strain, reserving the liquid. Put the carrots in a blender, cover with the cooking liquid, and blend until smooth, adding more of the liquid as necessary to get a soup with a consistency you like. Season and serve with crème fraîche. Serves 2.

Moroccan carrot and orange salad. Peel and slice 1 orange, then toss with Boiled carrots with caraway, sprinkling a pinch of ground cinnamon on top. Serves 2 as a side salad.

Caramelized carrots with butternut squash and star anise

Utterly delicious and full of flavor. The vegetables absorb the rich butter and flavors of star anise . . . inevitably becoming irresistible. Serves 4 to 5.

1 quantity Boiled carrots with caraway
7 oz [200 g] piece of butternut squash
Glug of light olive oil
4 Tbsp [50 g] butter
Small piece cinnamon stick or pinch of
  ground cinnamon
1 tsp cumin seeds
Sprig thyme
3 to 5 garlic cloves, to taste
3 star anise
3 to 4 sprigs flat-leaf parsley, roughly chopped

Preheat the oven to 350°F [180°C]. Cut the piece of butternut squash into wedges about the same thickness as the carrots.

Put the squash on a baking sheet with the light olive oil, salt, and pepper and turn to coat. Cover with foil and put in the oven 15 to 20 minutes, until just slightly soft.

Put a large, heavy-based skillet over medium heat and add the butter. Tip in the carrots and squash with the cinnamon, cumin, thyme, whole garlic cloves, and star anise. Reduce the heat and cook gently 15 minutes, turning occasionally. Sprinkle with the parsley and serve with salads, or grilled or roast meat or fish if you prefer.

STORAGE Both the boiled carrots and the squash dish will keep well in sealed containers in the refrigerator 3 days. Reheat both slowly in covered flameproof dishes on the stovetop, or in an oven preheated to 350°F [180°C], until piping hot.

EATING WINTER

apples and pears
beets
Brussels sprouts
cabbages
cauliflowers
celery
celery root
chestnuts
chicory
Jerusalem artichokes
kale
leeks
mushrooms (cultivated)
onions and shallots
oranges and other citrus
pak choi
parsnips
potatoes (main crop)
rhubarb
squashes and pumpkins
spinach
turnips and rutabaga

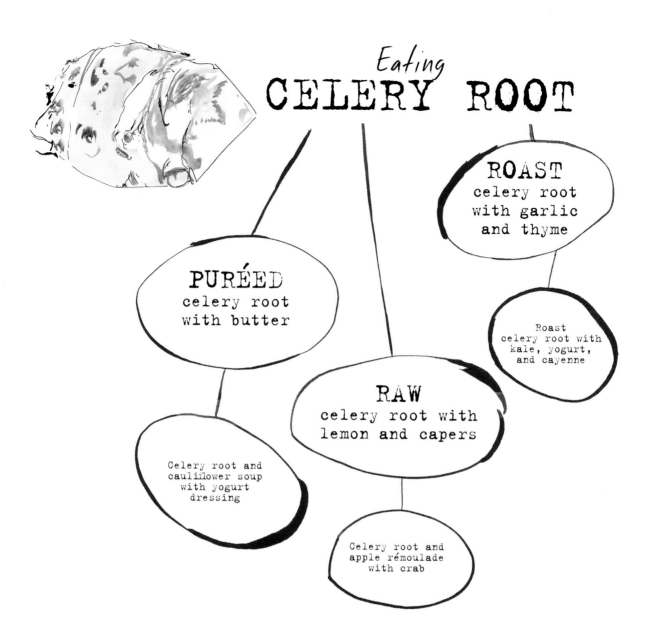

Eating
CELERY ROOT

ROAST
celery root
with garlic
and thyme

Roast
celery root with
kale, yogurt,
and cayenne

PURÉED
celery root
with butter

RAW
celery root with
lemon and capers

Celery root and
cauliflower soup
with yogurt
dressing

Celery root and
apple rémoulade
with crab

October to March Celery root takes the prize on my table during the winter months for being the ugliest (by quite some distance), yet tastiest vegetable. Try roasting it to bring out its intense nuttiness and anise aroma and serving it with crème fraîche (see page 134), or make a snowy white purée that is so rounded in flavor and sweet (see right). You can even eat celery root raw, thinly sliced into salads or made into a crunchy rémoulade (see page 137).

When preparing celery root, remember it can discolor quickly. This won't affect the flavor but, if you want to keep it white, put the prepared celery root in a bowl of water acidulated with a squeeze of lemon juice.

Choose a firm root that feels heavy for its size, as the center can become light and fluffy and unusable. Celery root keeps best in the refrigerator, although it will also be fine at room temperature. The tough skin is thick and needs to be removed, which can waste a lot of the root. Peel it with a serrated knife, removing any tough green flesh at the same time, then cut off the roots from the base.

Puréed celery root with butter

Celery root purée is ultimately decadent, rich, and smooth. It goes incredibly well with roast meat, especially lamb. Serves 4 as a side dish.

1 small celery root (1⅓ to 1¾ lb [600 to 800 g] unprepared weight), 3¾ cups [900 ml] whole cow's, goat's, or almond milk, ⅛ cup [25 g] butter (optional)

Prepare the celery root and cut the white flesh roughly into ¾ to 1 in [2 to 3 cm] cubes. Put into a small saucepan with the milk and bring to a boil, then reduce the heat to a low simmer 30 minutes. Check every now and then that the milk is not scorching on the base of the pan. Test the celery root by piercing it with a knife to see if it is soft. Let cool a little, then ladle into a blender with enough of the milk to make a thick purée (do not fill the blender more than about one-third full; work in batches if necessary). Make sure the lid is secured as the liquid is hot. Blend until very smooth. Return to the pan, add the butter, if using, and season.

MORE CELERY ROOT PURÉE . . . AND LEFTOVERS
With scallops. Hand-dived scallops are a little more expensive than others, but have much less impact on the sea bed than trawled scallops, and are of a higher quality. Heat a heavy-based skillet until it's really hot. Add a dash of light olive oil, then place the scallops in the pan. Sear 1 minute until they brown, then turn and repeat. Serve 3 scallops with a spoon of Puréed celery root with butter as a generous appetizer for one.

With shredded roast pork. Pork and celery root are a divine combination. After making a pork belly roast (see page 104), shred any leftovers. Reheat them in a sauté pan until crispy and hot and serve with Puréed celery root with butter.

Celery root and cauliflower soup with yogurt dressing

This snow-white soup is a warming bowlful that shows off two locally grown staples that, together, see us through the winter months. Serves 6 to 8.

1 quantity Puréed celery root with butter
1 leek, roughly chopped
1 onion, roughly sliced
Glug of light olive oil
3 garlic cloves, roughly chopped
1 small cauliflower
Whole cow's, goat's, or almond milk, if needed
Thick live natural yogurt
1 Tbsp cumin seeds, toasted (see page 163)

Sauté the leek and onion gently in the light olive oil 10 minutes until soft. Then add the garlic and sauté a further 5 minutes. Cut the cauliflower into florets, then peel the tough outer layer from the stalk and chop it. Keep any young leaves (compost large, tough leaves). Add the cauliflower and young leaves to the onion mixture.

Cover with water, bring to a boil, then reduce to a simmer and cook 15 minutes or until the cauliflower is soft. Ladle into a blender in small batches (so the blender is only about one-third full) and blend 1 to 2 minutes, or until smooth.

Return the soup to the pan, place over low heat, and season. Reheat the celery root purée over low heat in another pan, adding a little more milk if needed to get a soup consistency you like. When both are hot but not boiling, the soup is ready to serve. Half-fill wide bowls with the cauliflower soup, then ladle the celery root soup into the middle. Top with a spoon of yogurt and a sprinkling of toasted cumin seeds.

STORAGE Both the soup and the purée will keep well in sealed containers in the refrigerator 4 days. To serve, reheat gently until piping hot but not boiling.

Roast celery root with garlic and thyme

Roasting concentrates the nutty flavors of celery root, making it a particularly strong stand-alone—and deeply savory—vegetable that can make a meal. It works well as part of a potroast. Serves 4 as a side dish.

1 medium celery root (about 1¾ lb [800 g] unprepared weight), 12 garlic cloves (skin on), 4 sprigs thyme, glug of light olive oil, zest of ½ unwaxed lemon

Preheat the oven to 350°F [180°C]. Prepare the celery root, cut the white flesh into 2 in [5 cm] chunks, and place on a baking sheet. Add the garlic, thyme, oil, and grate over the lemon zest, then season and toss to cover the celery root in the oil and flavorings. Cover the sheet with foil and roast in the oven 25 minutes. Remove the foil, then roast a further 10 to 15 minutes, until the pieces of celery root color and become soft.

MORE ROAST CELERY ROOT . . . AND LEFTOVERS
Celery root dauphinoise. Preheat the oven to 350°F [180°C]. Mix 1 quantity Roast celery root with garlic and thyme (garlic cloves removed from their skins) with ⅝ cup [150 ml] heavy cream. Put on a small baking sheet or ovenproof dish so that it lies 1 to 2 in [2.5 to 5 cm] deep. Bake in the hot oven 25 minutes. Serves 4 as a side dish.

Kale crisps. If you have an abundance of kale, make umami-rich chips by drying the leaves. Preheat the oven to 350°F [180°C]. Pull the leaves from the stalks and cut in half. Drizzle with raw local honey and a little light olive oil, then sprinkle with sesame seeds and season with salt, massaging the dressing into the leaves. Spread out over baking sheets and put into the oven 15 minutes, then separate the leaves of kale and remove any that are already crispy. Return the rest to the oven another 5 minutes. Check, removing any more that are crisp, and repeat if necessary.

Roast celery root with kale, yogurt, and cayenne

This salad is absolutely full of flavor and is rather warming with the cayenne pepper. Serve as a light lunch or as part of a bigger evening meal with other wintry veg. Serves 6.

1 quantity Roast celery root with garlic and thyme, still warm
3½ oz [100 g] kale, stalks finely chopped, leaves roughly chopped
Juice of ½ lemon
½ cup [120 ml] thick live natural yogurt
2 tsp coriander seeds, toasted (see page 163) and crushed
Pinch of cayenne pepper
3 sprigs parsley, stalks finely chopped, leaves roughly chopped

Wash the kale, leaving a little water on the leaves to help them steam. Put them in a hot saucepan over medium heat and put the lid on. Stir occasionally, replacing the lid. After 5 minutes the kale should be wilted but still be bright green. Remove to a bowl.

Add the Roast celery root with garlic and thyme to the bowl with the lemon juice, toss with your hands, and taste for seasoning, then arrange on a serving plate.

Season the yogurt with the coriander seeds, salt, and pepper. Dress the salad plate with blobs of the yogurt and a dusting of cayenne pepper. Serve hot or cold, sprinkled with the parsley.

STORAGE Both the roast celery root and the salad will keep well in sealed containers in the refrigerator 3 days. Reheat the celery root in an oven preheated to 350°F [180°C] 15 minutes, or until hot right through. Return the salad to room temperature before serving.

Raw celery root with lemon and capers

Raw celery root is nutty and has a strong, uniquely earthy flavor. This simple dish goes well with fish. Serves 2 as a side salad.

5¼ oz [150 g] celery root (prepared weight), squeeze of lemon juice, 2 Tbsp salted capers, drained and rinsed

Cut the celery root into batons about 1/16 to ¼ in [3 to 5 mm] thick, adding them to a bowl and tossing with the lemon juice as you work, to stop them browning. Season with salt and pepper and mix in the capers.

MORE RAW CELERY ROOT . . . AND LEFTOVERS
Coleslaw. Mix 2¾ oz [75 g] leftover mayonnaise with 3½ oz [100 g] shredded cabbage, 1 grated carrot, ½ grated onion, and 2 Tbsp raisins. Serves 2 as a side salad.

Celery root and blue cheese muffins. Preheat the oven to 350°F [180°C]. Combine 1⅔ cups [200 g] spelt flour with 2 tsp baking powder, ½ tsp bicarbonate of soda, a pinch each of salt and pepper, 2 lightly beaten eggs, 1 cup [250 ml] live natural yogurt, and 1 quantity Raw celery root with lemon (omit the capers). Mix in 2¼ oz [60 g] crumbled blue cheese. Spoon into a buttered muffin pan and bake 15 to 18 minutes, until brown on top. Makes about 12.

Celery root and apple rémoulade with crab

This is my twist on the French classic, with apple for sweetness and the crab to make something special. The chili flakes bring the flavors together and give the dish a lift. Serves 4 as an appetizer.

For the salad
1 quantity Raw celery root with lemon and capers
1 tart eating apple, such as Cox's Orange Pippin, cut into batons the same size as the celery root
3½ oz [100 g] crab meat (optional)
Pinch of chili flakes

For the mayonnaise
1 large egg
Juice of ¼ lemon
1 tsp Dijon mustard
⅝ to ¾ cup [150 to 170 ml] flavorless vegetable oil

First make the mayonnaise. In a tall blender, blend all the ingredients except the oil. Then pour in the oil in a very slow, steady stream, blending constantly, until it forms a thick sauce. The mixture should be emulsified and creamy with a nice yellow tint. If it splits, remove from the blender, add a new egg yolk to the blender, turn it on, then slowly pour on the split mixture. Store in a sealed jar in the refrigerator.

Add the apple and half the crab (if using) to the Raw celery root with lemon and capers, then mix in half the mayonnaise (keep the other half in the jar in the refrigerator up to 4 days for general use).

Serve the rémoulade topped with the rest of the crab (if using) and the chili flakes, with crusty rye bread, or soudough bread, on the side.

STORAGE Mayonnaise will keep in a sealed jar in the refrigerator 4 days. The rémoulade is best eaten fresh, but will keep 3 days in a sealed container in the refrigerator.

COOK NATURAL We all know it's good to eat a balanced diet, but sometimes forget that this includes eating plenty of raw fruit and vegetables, even through the winter. Some are better for us when consumed raw, as this keeps certain nutrients, enzymes, and vitamins intact. For instance, beets have 25 percent more folate, a type of vitamin B, and red bell peppers have more vitamin C, when raw. I find that I have more energy when eating plenty of raw food, too.

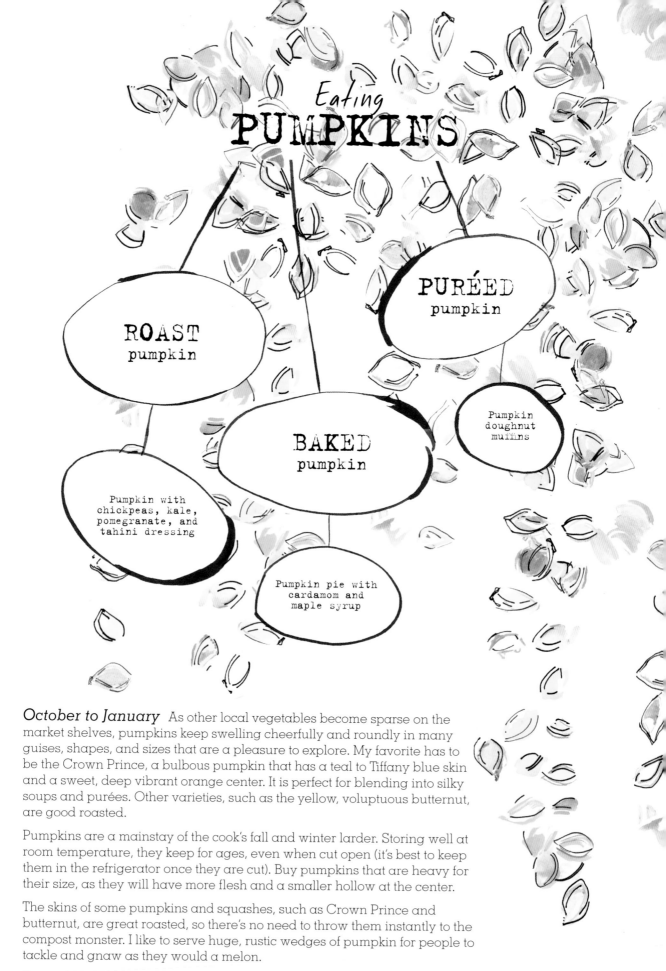

Eating
PUMPKINS

ROAST pumpkin

PURÉED pumpkin

BAKED pumpkin

Pumpkin with chickpeas, kale, pomegranate, and tahini dressing

Pumpkin doughnut muffins

Pumpkin pie with cardamom and maple syrup

October to January As other local vegetables become sparse on the market shelves, pumpkins keep swelling cheerfully and roundly in many guises, shapes, and sizes that are a pleasure to explore. My favorite has to be the Crown Prince, a bulbous pumpkin that has a teal to Tiffany blue skin and a sweet, deep vibrant orange center. It is perfect for blending into silky soups and purées. Other varieties, such as the yellow, voluptuous butternut, are good roasted.

Pumpkins are a mainstay of the cook's fall and winter larder. Storing well at room temperature, they keep for ages, even when cut open (it's best to keep them in the refrigerator once they are cut). Buy pumpkins that are heavy for their size, as they will have more flesh and a smaller hollow at the center.

The skins of some pumpkins and squashes, such as Crown Prince and butternut, are great roasted, so there's no need to throw them instantly to the compost monster. I like to serve huge, rustic wedges of pumpkin for people to tackle and gnaw as they would a melon.

Pumpkin seeds are easily made into a delightful snack. Dry them in the oven, then season with spices and butter and/or sweet maple syrup (see page 140).

Roast pumpkin

One of my favorite vegetables . . . and cooked in my favorite way. The edges of the pumpkin caramelize against the baking sheet and become so sweet and flavorful. Hunt for interesting pumpkin varieties to discover their subtly different textures, colors, and flavors. Serves 4 as a side dish.

1⅓ lb [600 g] pumpkin (unprepared weight),
light olive oil

Preheat the oven to 350°F [180°C]. Remove and reserve the pumpkin seeds (to roast them, see page 140) and cut the flesh into large wedges about 1 in [3 cm] thick. Lay on a baking sheet, season with salt and pepper, and drizzle with the oil, then turn over and season the other side. Cook in the oven 30 to 40 minutes. The pumpkin is ready when it has some color and is tender all the way through when pierced with a knife.

MORE ROAST PUMPKIN . . . AND LEFTOVERS
Spelt risotto. Gently sauté 1 finely chopped onion and 1 finely chopped garlic clove 5 minutes. Add 10½ oz [300 g] pearled spelt grains and stir 2 minutes. Cover with stock and allow to simmer and soak up the liquid, stirring. Repeat for 25 minutes, or until the spelt is almost cooked. Add 1 quantity Roast pumpkin, finely chopped. When the spelt is cooked, after another 5 minutes or so, add ⅔ cup [50 g] grated parmesan and a knob of butter. Serves 4.

Pomegranate juice. Knock the seeds out of the remaining half pomegranate (see right). Put them in a blender with a glass of water. Blend 1 minute, then strain through a nylon sieve and serve cold. Makes 1.

Pumpkin with chickpeas, kale, pomegranate, and tahini dressing

This is a salad full of stunning color and flavor that is always popular in the depths of winter. It keeps well, so can be made in advance. Serves 4 to 6.

For the salad
1 quantity Roast pumpkin
Glug of light olive oil
5¼ oz [150 g] kale or other winter greens, stalks finely chopped, leaves roughly chopped
1 garlic clove, chopped
½ pomegranate
3½ oz [100 g] cooked chickpeas, drained and rinsed (see page 155)

For the tahini dressing
1 Tbsp tahini
1 garlic clove, crushed
Squeeze of lemon juice

Heat the oil in a skillet that has a lid. Add the kale stalks and cook 2 minutes. Now add the leaves and garlic, put the lid on, and cook another 2 minutes. Season, then remove from the pan.

To remove the seeds from the half pomegranate, hold it over a bowl, round-side up. Hit it with a wooden spoon all over and let the seeds fall through your fingers and into the bowl.

Make the dressing: in a small bowl, mix the tahini, garlic, and lemon juice together. The mixture will become claggy. Add 1 Tbsp water and mix well to form a paste and remove any lumps. Then add another 1 Tbsp water and repeat until you have a smooth dressing with the consistency of heavy cream.

Mix the Roast pumpkin with the wilted kale and chickpeas and arrange the salad on a platter. Scatter with pomegranate seeds and drizzle with the tahini dressing to serve.

STORAGE The salad will keep 4 days in a sealed container in the refrigerator, though it is best left undressed and without the pomegranate if made in advance. Return it to room temperature before dressing, adding the pomegranate and serving.

Baked pumpkin

Use this sweet pumpkin recipe as a filling for pastries (try Olive oil pastry, see page 155), or even make a sweet pumpkin fool (see page 22, just replace the rhubarb in the recipe with Baked pumpkin). Serves 4.

1⅓ lb [600 g] pumpkin (unprepared weight), pinch of ground cinnamon, pinch of ground ginger, 6 cardamom pods, slightly crushed, 3½ Tbsp [50 ml] maple syrup or raw local honey

Preheat the oven to 350°F [180°C]. Cut the pumpkin into wedges 1 to 2 in [3 to 5 cm] thick. Reserve the seeds to roast later (see below). Place the pumpkin wedges on a baking sheet, sprinkle with the spices, and drizzle the syrup or honey over the top. Cover with foil and bake 40 to 50 minutes, or until the pumpkin is very soft. Remove the foil and let cool a little. Scrape the pumpkin flesh from the skins back onto the sheet with the sweet spicy juices. Mash together with the juices using a fork (shred and compost the skins). Spread on toast for breakfast, or make into pie or pancakes (see below).

MORE BAKED PUMPKIN . . . AND LEFTOVERS
Maple-roasted pumpkin seeds. Preheat the oven to 300°F [150°C]. Wash the seeds, then dry with a dish towel. Spread out on a sheet of baking parchment on a baking sheet and dry in the oven 30 minutes. Drizzle with maple syrup, return to the oven, and allow to dry and caramelize once more. Watch carefully, as they scorch easily.

Pumpkin pancakes. Mix together 1¼ cups [150 g] spelt flour, ½ tsp bicarbonate of soda, 2 tsp baking powder, 14 Tbsp [200 ml] natural live yogurt, 7 Tbsp [100 ml] whole milk, 2 eggs, and 7 oz [200 g] Baked pumpkin. Heat a heavy-based pan with a drop of flavorless vegetable oil. Drop in a spoon of the batter and allow it to spread. Fill the pan with pancakes, giving each a little space. Cook one side until lightly browned and the top bubbles, then flip. Cook the other side evenly. Serve hot with maple syrup. Serves 4 to 6.

Pumpkin martini. Mix 1 quantity Baked pumpkin with a 4½ cups [1 L] bottle of vodka in a large jar or bowl and seal. Leave for anything from 1 day to 2 weeks in the refrigerator. To make a pumpkin martini for one, mix 3½ Tbsp [50 ml] of the strained vodka with 2 tsp Cointreau and serve over ice.

Pumpkin pie with cardamom and maple syrup

This is a healthy classic and so tasty. I can't get enough of the nut base; if you have any spare, roll it into balls and eat them as energy snacks. Serves 8.

For the filling
1 quantity Baked pumpkin
3 eggs, lightly beaten
14 Tbsp [200 ml] heavy cream
Handful of Maple-roasted pumpkin seeds (see below left)

For the crust
1 cup [100 g] walnuts or pecans
1 cup [100 g] almonds
1¼ cup [100 g] rolled oats
10½ oz [300 g] dates

Preheat the oven to 325°F [160°C]. First make the crust: blend the nuts, oats, and dates until they are fine and sticky. Add 2 Tbsp water and pulse-blend a few times, until mixed. Remove from the blender and mix by hand.

Line a 9 to 10 in [22 to 25 cm] tart case with foil and press the crust firmly into the case.

Mix the Baked pumpkin with the eggs and cream and pour the mixture into the tart case. Bake 35 minutes, or until it sets.

Serve the tart with ice cream or whipped cream and a sprinkle of Maple-roasted pumpkin seeds (see left).

STORAGE Both the baked pumpkin and the pie will keep well 4 days in a sealed container in the refrigerator. Return to room temperature to serve.

COOK NATURAL I like to pack my desserts with fruit and to use less flour and sugar. This recipe, and the Pumpkin doughnut muffins overleaf, are good examples. But also think outside the box in the colder months and include fruits in savory dishes, or vegetables in baked goods: check out the Celery root and blue cheese muffins (see page 137) and the Rhubarb and pork tagine (see page 19). During the winter, the seasonal cook becomes more dependent on legumes, canned and dried foods, root veg, and winter greens, so this is where real creativity starts to happen as we invent these interesting new dishes with our more limited array of fruits and vegetables.

Puréed pumpkin

This sweet purée is good on a plate with roast pork, or stirred through a whole grain risotto with crisp bacon lardoons and chopped sage. Serves 2 as a side dish.

7 oz [200 g] pumpkin (unprepared weight)

Peel the pumpkin with a sharp knife or a vegetable peeler. Remove the seeds with a spoon and reserve (see page 140), then cut the pumpkin roughly into ¾ to 1 in [2 to 3 cm] pieces. Place in a small saucepan and cover with water, bring to a boil, then reduce the heat and simmer 10 to 15 minutes until soft. Strain and reserve the liquid. Put the pumpkin in a blender (make sure it is not more than one-third full) and blend to a purée, adding a little of the cooking liquid to help it become smooth.

MORE PURÉED PUMPKIN . . . AND LEFTOVERS
Pumpkin trifle. Whisk 7 oz [200 g] cream cheese with 1 quantity Puréed pumpkin, ½ tsp ground cinnamon, and ½ tsp allspice. Whip 1 cup [250 ml] heavy cream with ½ cup [100 g] rapadura or raw cane sugar to form soft peaks. Fold half the sweetened cream into the pumpkin mixture. Crush 6 of your favorite cookies and distribute half the crumbs between 5 glasses. Top with a spoon of pumpkin, then layer with more cookie crumbs, followed by the rest of the pumpkin, then finish with a spoon of cream. Refrigerate and serve on the same day. Serves 5.

Pumpkin and ginger soup. Add enough of the cooking liquid to 1 quantity Puréed pumpkin to make a soup of the consistency you like. Season with a pinch of ground ginger, salt, and pepper. To serve, reheat to just below boiling. Serves 2.

Pumpkin doughnut muffins

These delicious little muffins are made from a simple variation on a doughnut batter that tastes divine rolled in cinnamon sugar. Baking them in the oven is both much healthier and simpler than deep-frying. The pumpkin gives them an appetizing orange color and keeps them nice and moist. Makes about 12.

1 quantity Puréed pumpkin
⅓ cup [75 g] soft butter, plus more for the pan and to brush
1½ cups [180 g] spelt flour, plus more for the pan
5 Tbsp [75 g] rapadura or raw cane sugar, plus more to coat
1 large egg, lightly beaten
1½ tsp baking powder
¼ tsp bicarbonate of soda
½ tsp allspice (optional)
3 Tbsp natural live yogurt
1 tsp ground cinnamon

Preheat the oven to 350°F [180°C]. Butter 12 hollows of a muffin pan, then sprinkle with flour and turn the pan, tapping, so the hollows are well floured.

Beat the butter and sugar for a few minutes until light and fluffy. Add the egg, flour, baking powder, bicarbonate of soda, allspice (if using), yogurt, and pumpkin and stir together until thoroughly mixed.

Fill the muffin molds half full, then bake 20 to 25 minutes until springy. Turn out of the pan. Immediately melt a little butter and, as soon as the muffins are cool enough to handle, brush the tops with butter, then roll in a plate of sugar mixed with the cinnamon.

STORAGE The muffins are best warm from the oven, but will keep 3 days in an airtight container. The purée will keep 3 days in a sealed container in the refrigerator; reheat it gently in a covered saucepan on the stovetop, with a splash of water added.

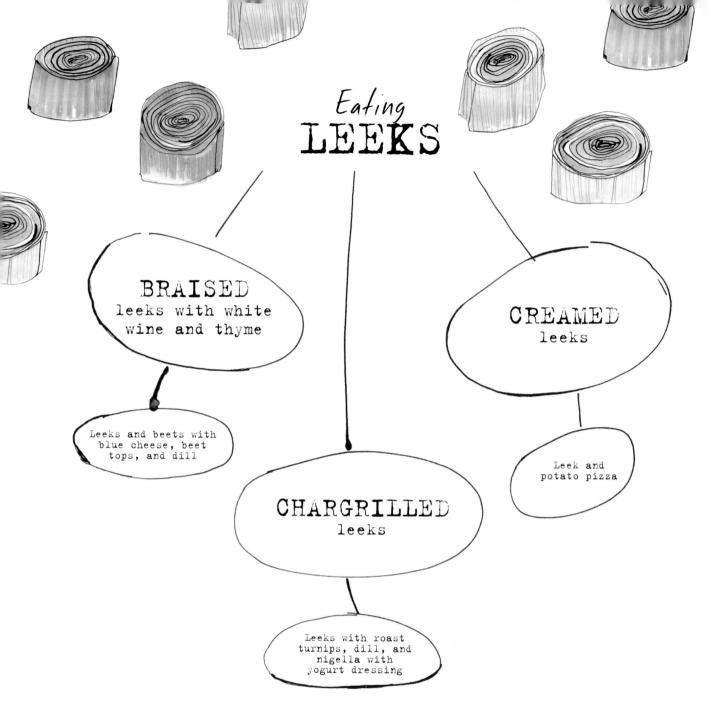

Eating LEEKS

BRAISED
leeks with white wine and thyme

Leeks and beets with blue cheese, beet tops, and dill

CHARGRILLED
leeks

Leeks with roast turnips, dill, and nigella with yogurt dressing

CREAMED
leeks

Leek and potato pizza

September to March Leeks are one of our main winter crops and keep us going through the coldest months. They don't only have to be used in standard soups, stocks, and stews, however comforting those might be. Experiment with this earthy vegetable and discover your own treatments. Try leeks as they are here, in new guises: chargrilled in salads (see page 149), on pizza with potatoes (see page 146), or braised with wine and herbs (see right).

Buy leeks that are a vibrant green, firm, and crisp. Small leeks are better for chargrilling, while big leeks are good for stews and braising. Leeks keep well at room temperature, but will last a bit longer if stored in the refrigerator.

The green tops are earthy and tough, but still full of flavor. Compost only the very darkest green tops, chop the rest finely, and cook it all alongside the lighter green-and-white stem, or use the dark green parts in stocks and broths.

Braised leeks with white wine and thyme

Leeks take well to braising, becoming soft, savory, and sweet. Serve these with most meals, or make into cooked salads. Serves 4 as a side dish.

14 oz [400 g] leeks, 2 garlic cloves, 3 to 4 sprigs thyme, splash of white wine, 4 Tbsp [50 g] butter

Preheat the oven to 350°F [180°C]. Remove the roots and cut the leeks into 2 in [5 cm] pieces. Rinse them, being careful to remove any mud from the layers of the upper stalk. Keep the darkest green tops for a stock, as they taste a bit too earthy to eat alone. Fill a baking sheet with the leeks. Chop the garlic and scatter it over the leeks with the thyme and wine. Cut or pinch the butter into smaller pieces and place some on each bit of leek. Cover with foil and put in the oven 35 to 40 minutes, shaking the sheet halfway through the cooking time.

MORE BRAISED LEEKS . . . AND LEFTOVERS
Leek and blue cheese tart. Make a vegetarian version of the Spinach and smoked fish tart recipe (see page 151), replacing the spinach and fish mixture with 1 quantity Braised leeks with white wine and thyme and 3½ oz [100 g] crumbled blue cheese. Serves 4.

Leek and pollack gratin. Preheat the oven to 350°F [180°C]. Cut 10½ oz [300 g] pollack into small cubes. Mix with 1 quantity Braised leeks with white wine and thyme, 1¾ oz [50 g] crumbled blue cheese, and 7 Tbsp [100 ml] heavy cream. Put the mixture into an ovenproof dish and sprinkle with brown breadcrumbs. Bake 25 to 30 minutes until piping hot. Serves 4.

Leeks and beets with blue cheese, beet tops, and dill

A robust winter salad that packs a punch. Serve this as an appetizer or hearty lunch with some bread. It can be served warm but, if you want to serve it cold, allow the beets, leaves, and leeks to cool down before mixing them with the other ingredients. Serves 4.

1 quantity **Braised leeks with white wine and thyme**
2 beets (about 14 oz [400 g])
The beet tops, or 1¾ oz [50 g] spinach or chard
Light olive oil
1 tsp dill seeds or ½ tsp caraway seeds
1¾ oz [50 g] Stilton or Stichelton, crumbled
3 sprigs dill, stalks finely chopped, fronds
  roughly chopped

Preheat the oven to 350°F [180°C]. Prepare the beets: remove the beet tops and rinse them, composting any yellow leaves. Remove the rough skin at the top of the beets and cut into wedges. Put the beets on a baking sheet, toss in light olive oil, salt, and pepper, then cover with foil. Put in the oven 30 minutes. Remove the foil, turn the beets, and return to the oven another 20 to 30 minutes. When they are soft and have caramelized in places, they are ready.

Chop the stalks of the beet tops or greens finely and shred the leaves. Fry the stalks, leaves, and dill seeds in a little of the oil from the beet tray ¾ a couple of minutes, to wilt the leaves and soften the stalks.

When you are ready to serve, combine the beets, beet leaves, and leeks with the crumbled cheese and dill. Turn to mix just 2 or 3 times, so that each ingredient is still visible. Serve hot or cold.

STORAGE Both the braised leeks and the salad will keep 4 days in sealed containers in the refrigerator. Reheat the leeks, covered, in an oven preheated to 350°F [180°C], until hot right through. Return the salad to room temperature before serving.

Creamed leeks

A rich comforting treat, excellent with a pot roast. Serves 4 as a side dish.

14 oz [400 g] leeks, 4 Tbsp [50 g] butter, 2 garlic cloves, 3 Tbsp white wine (optional), ⅓ cup [80 ml] heavy cream

Slice the leeks into ⅜ in [1 cm] pieces, using everything but the very darkest tops (compost those). Wash thoroughly. Heat a large skillet over medium heat, add the butter and the leeks, and sauté 10 minutes until soft. Roughly chop the garlic, add it to the pan, and sauté a further 2 minutes, then add the wine (if using), or 3 Tbsp water, and allow it to boil 2 minutes. Reduce the heat and add the cream. Stir occasionally 10 minutes, until the leeks are soft and the sauce has thickened.

MORE CREAMED LEEKS . . . AND LEFTOVERS
Buckwheat pancakes. Mix ¾ cup [100 g] buckwheat flour with 1 lightly beaten egg, 1 cup [250 ml] milk and a pinch of salt. Rest in the refrigerator 30 minutes. Fry in an oiled pan like a regular pancake. Serve stuffed with leftover Creamed leeks and grated cheddar cheese. Serves 4.

Leek and potato soup. Blend leftover boiled potatoes with leftover Creamed leeks and a little water for a quick, rich soup.

Leek and potato pizza

This is a twist on the classic potato pizza bianca, rather comically inspired by leek and potato soup. It works really well. It's very rich; the cream makes up for the lack of mozzarella. Makes 1 large pizza.

For the topping
1 quantity Creamed leeks
2 potatoes (about 10½ oz [300 g]), sliced ¼ in [5 mm] thick
3 sprigs rosemary, needles picked

For the spelt pizza dough
1¼ cups [150 g] spelt flour, or strong white flour, plus more to dust
½ tsp dried yeast
1 tsp fine salt
Glug of extra virgin olive oil, plus more for the topping
A little light olive oil

First make the dough. Mix all the ingredients except the light olive oil together with 7 Tbsp [100 ml] warm water. Cover with a clean plastic bag and set aside to rest 30 minutes. Knead the dough 5 minutes, then rest for 1½ hours to prove in a warm place.

When ready to cook, preheat the oven to its maximum temperature for a good 15 minutes, so that it's really hot. Boil the potatoes about 5 minutes, until they just soften. Drain and allow to dry. Toss with a splash of extra virgin oil, salt, pepper, and the rosemary.

Oil a baking sheet with the regular light olive oil. Roll out the dough ¹⁄₁₆ to ¼ in [3 to 5 mm] thick on a lightly floured work surface, or to the rough size of the sheet. Fill the sheet with the dough. Spread with the Creamed leeks, then place the rosemary and potatoes evenly on top. Drizzle with extra virgin oil and bake 25 to 30 minutes, or until the base has browned and is cooked through.

STORAGE The pizza is good eaten fresh, but is also great served cold for breakfast.

COOK NATURAL Spelt is an ancient grain that is more nutritious and digestible than regular wheat. Even those without an intolerance to wheat will feel the benefits of using spelt flour. It has a delicious nutty flavor and is easy to work with. It can be used to replace wheat flour in any recipe and works really well in pastries and bread. It is also savory and scrumptious as a whole grain used in pilafs and as an alternative to risotto rice (see pages 139 and 149 for recipes).

WINTER GREENS
Eating

STEAMED
spinach

Spinach and
smoked
fish tart

BLANCHED
chard with olive
oil and garlic

Spanakopita

RAW
kale with
sesame seeds
and honey

Kale and
kohlrabi
kimchi

October to February Kale and chard are my favorite winter vegetables. Each time I eat them, I feel physically healthier and full of energy. We're spoiled for choice these days with all sorts of varieties, from the purple Russian kale—my favorite salad leaf—via cavolo nero, the amazing black kale originally from Tuscany but now grown locally, to rainbow chard with its fabulous eye-popping colors. All these varieties are found in markets now without too much difficulty.

Buy smaller leaves for salads but, for cooking, large leaves are tastier and rich in iron. Look for fresh leaves that will be perky and squeakily crisp. Leafy greens often have a high level of pesticide residues, so buy organic when possible. Store, unwashed, in a plastic bag in the refrigerator.

Steamed spinach

A quick no-nonsense way to cook spinach that can be served at any time, from breakfast with eggs, through lunch with pasta, or with your evening meal. Serves 4 as a side dish.

8¾ oz [250 g] spinach, extra virgin olive oil

If the spinach has thick stalks, remove them and chop them finely. Chop the spinach leaves into 2 or 3 depending how big they are. Heat a skillet that has a lid over medium heat. Meanwhile, wash the spinach, then allow to drain a little, leaving some water on the leaves to help steam it in the pan. Add the spinach stalks and leaves to the pan and season with a little salt, pepper, and dash of the extra virgin oil. Put the lid on and allow to steam 2 or 3 minutes. Remove the lid and turn the spinach to cover in the oil and ensure it has wilted evenly.

MORE STEAMED SPINACH . . . AND LEFTOVERS
Beef and spinach empanadas. Make a batch of Olive oil pastry (see page 155). Preheat the oven to 350°F [180°C]. Fry 7 oz [200 g] ground beef in light olive oil with 1 finely chopped chili and a pinch of allspice until cooked through and browned. Mix with 1 quantity Steamed spinach. Divide the pastry into 9 balls, then roll each out into a 4 in [10 cm] disc. Put some spinach and beef filling in the middle. Brush the edges with milk, fold over to make a half circle, and seal the edges with a fork. Bake in the hot oven 25 to 30 minutes. Makes 9.

Creamed spinach. Add a dash of heavy cream, a grating of nutmeg, and a knob of butter to 1 quantity Steamed spinach at the end of cooking, then increase the heat a little. Turn the spinach in the cream and allow it to evaporate and thicken. When the sauce is thick, it is ready. Serves 4 as a side dish.

Spinach and smoked fish tart

This is real comfort food and is so worth the effort. If you don't eat fish, or don't want to use it, add 7 oz [200 g] crumbled feta instead. Serves 4.

1 quantity Steamed spinach
2 small onions, finely sliced
Glug of light olive oil
7 oz [200 g] hot-smoked trout or mackerel
⅔ cup [50 g] mature cheddar cheese, grated
8 in [20 cm] blind-baked shortcrust pastry case
  (see page 28)
3 small eggs, lightly beaten
⅝ cup [150 ml] heavy cream
⅝ cup [150 ml] milk

Preheat the oven to 340°F [170°C]. Sauté the onions in the light olive oil 10 minutes until soft. Squeeze out any juices from the Steamed spinach, or they will make the tart wet.

Flake the fish into a bowl and add the cheese, onions, and spinach. Mix and season to taste. Spread loosely into the tart case.

Whisk the eggs with the cream and milk. Season and pour over the fish filling. Bake 35 to 40 minutes, until just set in the middle (test by wobbling it).

STORAGE Both the spinach and the tart will keep 4 days in sealed containers in the refrigerator. Reheat the spinach in a pan over high heat, adding a splash of oil if needed. Return the tart to room temperature before serving, or reheat it in an oven preheated to 350°F [180°C] until hot right through.

COOK NATURAL The stalks of greens are full of fiber and are very nutritious, so why throw them away? Cooking with the stalks, you also get more bang for your buck. Sometimes they can be a little tough, but they are still delicious. Finely chop the larger stalks and cook just a couple of minutes longer than the leaves; they taste great and add texture to any dish.

Raw kale with sesame seeds and honey

Massaging lemon, honey, and salt into the kale helps to soften the leaves and gives it a great flavor. Serves 6 to 8 as a side salad.

14 oz [400 g] kale, juice of ½ lemon, 1 Tbsp raw local honey, ¾ to 1 in [2 to 3 cm] piece of ginger root, 2 Tbsp sesame seeds, extra virgin olive oil (optional)

Pull the kale leaves off the thick stalks. Finely chop the stalks and roughly chop the leaves, then wash both. Drain well, then put in a bowl with 1 tsp salt, the lemon juice, and honey. Massage the dressing into the leaves for 2 to 3 minutes, bruising them so they soak up the juices. Leave for 30 minutes, then pour off the excess liquid. Finely chop the ginger and add it with the sesame seeds. Mix and dress with extra virgin oil, if you like.

MORE RAW KALE . . . AND LEFTOVERS
Pulled pork and kimchi slider. This combo has to be tried! If you roast some pork, it's worth making more than you need so you've got some for this dish. Shred leftover pork and reheat it in a skillet until hot right through. Serve in a warmed burger bun with a spoon of kimchi on top.

Kimchi rice. If you need to use up your kimchi, boil 5¼ oz [150 g] brown rice until soft, then drain. Fry a couple of spoons of kimchi in a pan with a little flavorless oil. After a few minutes, add the drained rice to the skillet and cook them together until piping hot. I like to top each portion with a fried egg. Serves 2.

Kale and kohlrabi kimchi

Homemade kimchi is wonderful, with the added bonus of containing probiotics from the fermentation process (it won't contain these if you don't let it ferment), so it is good for gut flora. It is full of good bacteria that help keep your immune system healthy. The Koreans commonly use cabbage to make kimchi, so feel free to substitute that if you prefer. Fills one 4½ cup [1 L] tub.

1 quantity Raw kale with sesame seeds and honey
4 Tbsp rice flour, or spelt or all-purpose flour will do
8 garlic cloves
1 onion, roughly chopped
3½ Tbsp [50 ml] fish sauce
4 Tbsp Korean chili powder, or 2 Tbsp cayenne pepper
1 small kohlrabi (about 8¾ oz [250 g]), peeled and cut into ¾ in [5 mm] matchsticks
1 carrot, cut into ¾ in [5 mm] matchsticks
1 leek, thinly sliced
Sesame seeds, to serve (optional)

Bring 1⅔ cups [400 ml] water to a gentle simmer with the rice flour. Keep stirring for a few minutes until it thickens and starts to bubble. Simmer another 1 or 2 minutes until it becomes like an opaque oatmeal.

Blend the garlic, onion, and fish sauce to a purée. Transfer to a bowl, add the flour mixture and chili powder, and mix. Then add the kohlrabi, carrot, and leek, and finally the Raw kale with sesame seeds and honey. Mix well.

Put into a sterilized nonmetallic tub (see page 52), such as a Tupperware box, and press down to pack it in. Put the lid on. Eat it fresh with sesame seeds sprinkled on top, or leave it at cool room temperature 2 to 3 days. After 2 days, check if you can see any tiny bubbles; they will prove it is fermenting. If not, leave it out of the refrigerator a little longer, until the fermentation process starts.

STORAGE Keep the kimchi in a sealed, nonmetallic container in the refrigerator and eat within 3 weeks. The raw kale is best eaten immediately.

Blanched chard with olive oil and garlic

This dish is a real treat and so simple, though a good extra virgin olive oil is essential for flavor. You must be careful when cooking with extra virgin oil not to heat it to smoking point—that will ruin the flavor and saturate the fats—so cook it over low heat. Serves 4 as a side dish.

10½ oz [300 g] chard, glug of extra virgin olive oil, 1 garlic clove

Boil a large pan of salted water. Wash the chard, then drop it into the boiling water in batches for 30 seconds. Pick out with tongs, shake dry, and put on a baking sheet. Allow the water to return to a boil between each batch. When all the chard has been blanched, pour off any excess water from the sheet. Finely slice the garlic. Heat the olive oil and add the garlic. When the oil begins to bubble around the garlic, add the chard. Turn the chard in the oil and warm through to serve.

MORE BLANCHED CHARD . . . AND LEFTOVERS

Chard with anchovies and chili. Make 1 quantity Blanched chard with olive oil and garlic, but add 4 chopped anchovies and a pinch of chili flakes at the same time as the garlic. Serves 4 as a side dish; excellent with fish or lamb.

Chard with chickpeas and tomato. Soak 3½ oz [100 g] dried chickpeas overnight, then drain and cover with fresh water. Add 1 bay leaf and ½ onion and boil about 50 minutes until soft. Drain, remove the bay and onion, and mix the chickpeas with 1 quantity Blanched chard with olive oil and garlic. Season with a squeeze of lemon juice. Serves 6 as a side dish or as part of a mixed meze.

Spanakopita

A delicious Greek pie that has the country's essential herbal triad of dill, parsley, and mint. Together, these create an amazing, unique flavor. This is a vegan version with no feta, but feel free to add 5¼ oz [150 g] feta, crumbled into the filling, if you like. If you don't want to make your own pastry, use filo. Makes 9.

For the spanakopita
1 quantity Blanched chard with olive oil and garlic, cut into rough pieces
3 onions, sliced
Light olive oil
3 garlic cloves, roughly chopped
6 sprigs dill, finely chopped
6 sprigs parsley, finely chopped
6 sprigs mint, finely chopped
Nutmeg, grated, to taste
Finely grated unwaxed lemon zest, to taste
2 Tbsp sesame seeds

For the olive oil pastry
2 cups [250 g] spelt or all-purpose flour, plus more to dust
¼ cup [60 ml] light olive oil, plus more to brush

To make the pastry, put the flour in a bowl with the olive oil, ½ cup [120 ml] cold water and a pinch of salt. Mix until combined, then knead 5 to 10 minutes. Set aside to rest 30 minutes.

Meanwhile, sauté the onions in the light olive oil in a heavy-based skillet 15 minutes. Add the garlic and cook 2 minutes, then add the dill, parsley, and mint. Cook 2 more minutes, then remove from the heat and stir in the Blanched chard with olive oil and garlic. Season with salt, pepper, nutmeg, and lemon zest to taste. Preheat the oven to 375°F [190°C].

Divide the pastry into nine balls. Roll each out into a 12 in [5 cm] round on a lightly floured surface. Now put 3 heaped Tbsp of filling in the middle of each, brush the rim with water, and fold 3 equally spaced points from the edge to the middle to meet and form a pyramid shape. Seal the seams by pressing them tightly together. Brush the tops with olive oil, then sprinkle with the sesame seeds. Bake the pies 30 minutes, until golden brown.

STORAGE Both the blanched chard and the pies will keep in sealed containers in the refrigerator 4 days. Reheat the chard in a skillet. Eat the spanakopita at room temperature, or reheat in an oven preheated to 350°F [180°C] until hot right through.

Eating TURNIPS

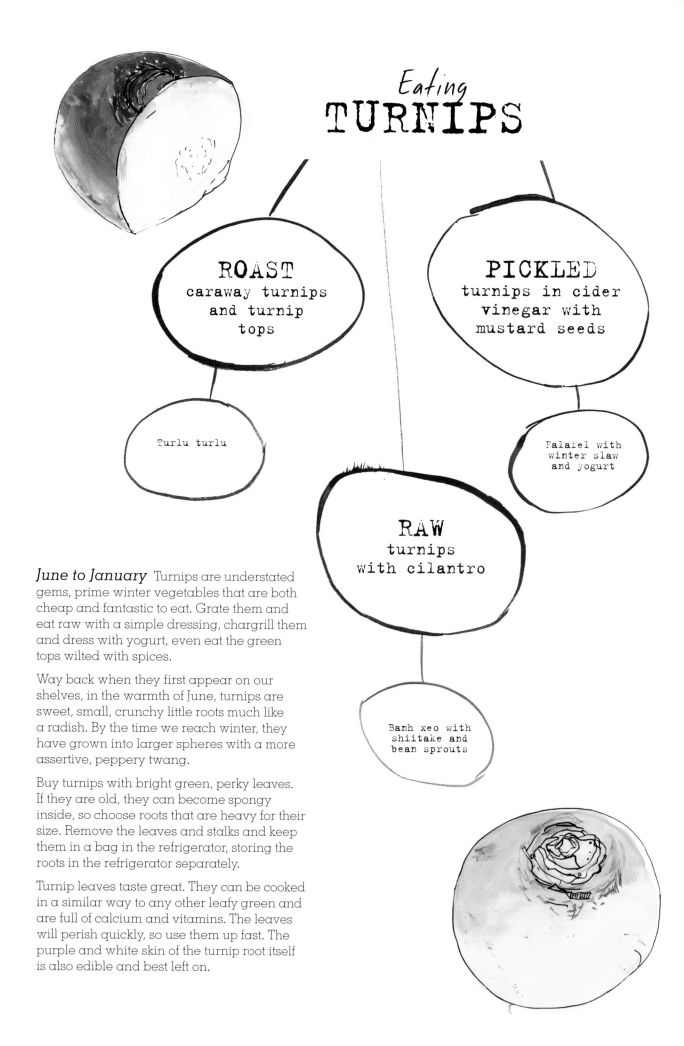

ROAST
caraway turnips
and turnip
tops

> Turlu turlu

PICKLED
turnips in cider
vinegar with
mustard seeds

> Falafel with
> winter slaw
> and yogurt

RAW
turnips
with cilantro

> Banh xeo with
> shiitake and
> bean sprouts

June to January Turnips are understated gems, prime winter vegetables that are both cheap and fantastic to eat. Grate them and eat raw with a simple dressing, chargrill them and dress with yogurt, even eat the green tops wilted with spices.

Way back when they first appear on our shelves, in the warmth of June, turnips are sweet, small, crunchy little roots much like a radish. By the time we reach winter, they have grown into larger spheres with a more assertive, peppery twang.

Buy turnips with bright green, perky leaves. If they are old, they can become spongy inside, so choose roots that are heavy for their size. Remove the leaves and stalks and keep them in a bag in the refrigerator, storing the roots in the refrigerator separately.

Turnip leaves taste great. They can be cooked in a similar way to any other leafy green and are full of calcium and vitamins. The leaves will perish quickly, so use them up fast. The purple and white skin of the turnip root itself is also edible and best left on.

Roast caraway turnips and turnip tops

Turnips are so neglected; the roots are sweet, peppery, and delicious. Roasting is a good method to use with turnips, as it brings out their sweetness. This could accompany any meal, from a pot roast to a meze of salads. Serves 4 as a side dish.

10½ oz [300 g] turnips, 1 tsp caraway seeds, 1 tsp cumin seeds, light olive oil

Preheat the oven to 350°F [180°C]. Wash the turnips, then remove any leaves and set aside. Cut the turnips into wedges about ¾ in [2 cm] thick. Lay them on a baking sheet, season with salt and pepper and the caraway and cumin seeds and drizzle with the oil, then toss to cover them evenly. Put into the oven 20 minutes, turn them, then return to the oven another 20 minutes. They are ready when they have some color and are tender when pierced with a knife. Wilt any turnip tops in a skillet with a drizzle more olive oil and a little seasoning for 2 minutes. Stir them into the roast turnips and serve.

MORE ROAST TURNIPS . . . AND LEFTOVERS
Turnips with nuts, yogurt, and parsley. If you have any leftover Roast caraway turnips and turnip tops, make this amazing salad. Mix in a generous pinch of chopped flat-leaf parsley and a spoon or two of natural live yogurt, enough to coat the turnips. Crush 2 Tbsp nuts—walnuts, almonds, or hazelnuts will do—and sprinkle on top.

Roast turnips with parmesan. Make 1 quantity Roast caraway turnips and turnip tops. When they are ready, put them in an ovenproof dish, sprinkle with ⅔ cup [50 g] grated parmesan and return to the oven 5 minutes to melt the cheese. Serve hot as part of a veggie meal, or with chicken or fish if you like. Serves 4 as a side dish.

Turlu turlu

This dish is normally made from summer vegetables, but works just as well with winter produce. It's a bit like a Turkish-style ratatouille. Serves 4.

1 quantity Roast caraway turnips and
  turnip tops, assembled but not yet cooked
1 red onion, cut into wedges
5¼ oz [150 g] carrots, cut in half lengthwise, then cut into
  2 in [5 cm] lengths
5¼ oz [150 g] potato, cut into ⅜ in [1 cm] thick slices
Light olive oil
1 tsp coriander seeds
6 garlic cloves
14 oz [400 g] can of tomatoes
3½ oz [100 g] cooked chickpeas (see page 155), drained
  and rinsed
3 sprigs cilantro, finely chopped
3 sprigs parsley, finely chopped

Preheat the oven to 350°F [180°C]. Toss the red onion, carrots, and potato in the olive oil, coriander seeds, and garlic and roast 10 minutes, then add the turnips and continue to cook 40 minutes, turning everything halfway through. Stir occasionally until all is cooked and has taken on some color.

Add the tomatoes, chickpeas, and half the herbs. Mix and return to the oven 10 minutes.

Finish by seasoning with salt and pepper and top with the remaining herbs.

STORAGE Both the roast turnips and the turlu turlu will keep in sealed containers in the refrigerator 5 days. Reheat both in an oven preheated to 350°F [180°C] until hot right through.

COOK NATURAL The ugly, the unwanted, and the unloved. Many of the less attractive root veggies such as turnips, celery root, rutabaga, kohlrabi, and Jerusalem artichokes don't sell well, but they all taste delicious and are usually pretty cheap. I like to make the most of them and learn inspiring ways to cook them from around the world. I hope these recipes will convert the hardest skeptic.

Raw turnips with cilantro

This is a surprisingly sweet and simple salad that will freshen up any meal. It works really well with oily fish, such as fried mackerel fillets with soy sauce. Serve with a wedge of lime, so that people can dress the salad themselves. Serves 4 as a side salad.

10½ oz [300 g] turnips, 5 sprigs cilantro, 1 tsp black onion (nigella) or mustard seeds, ½ tsp toasted sesame oil (optional), lime wedges

First wash the turnips, top and tail them, and peel only if they have a tough skin. Grate them coarsely. Finely chop the stalks of the cilantro and roughly chop the leaves. Put the cilantro in a bowl with the turnips. Just before serving, toss with the black onion seeds or mustard seeds, a pinch of salt, and the sesame oil, if using. Serve with the lime wedges.

MORE RAW TURNIPS . . . AND LEFTOVERS
Turnip latkes. Make 1 quantity Raw turnips with cilantro (omitting the sesame oil). Squeeze out as much of the juice as you can from the mixture and put into a bowl. Mix in 2 Tbsp wholewheat or spelt flour and 1 lightly beaten egg. Place a skillet over medium heat and add a little flavorless vegetable oil. Fry spoonfuls of the latke mixture until golden brown, then flip and brown the other side. Serve with sour cream or mustard. Serves 4 as a snack.

Grated turnip with apple and walnut. Make 1 quantity Raw turnips with cilantro (omitting the sesame oil), add 1 grated apple and ½ cup [50 g] crushed walnuts. Dress with olive oil at the last minute. Serves 4 as a crunchy, refreshing side dish.

Banh xeo with shiitake and bean sprouts

Banh xeo are a type of Vietnamese pancake. They're a challenge to make, but fun, and the flavor makes it worthwhile. They are traditionally made with shrimp and pork, but shiitake mushrooms and raw turnip salad make a delicious veggie alternative. Makes 8.

For the filling
1 quantity Raw turnips with cilantro
Drizzle of flavorless vegetable oil
4¼ to 5¼ oz [120 to 150 g] shiitake mushrooms, finely sliced
½ leek, finely sliced
7 oz [200 g] bean sprouts
3 sprigs mint
Romaine lettuce leaves

For the pancakes
¾ cup [100 g] rice flour (available in most grocery stores but ask in an Asian store to get the best type for this dish)
½ tsp turmeric
1 cup [250 ml] coconut milk, chilled
Flavorless vegetable oil

For the dipping sauce
Juice of 1 lime
2 Tbsp fish sauce (optional, if not using, add salt to taste)
2 tsp rapadura or raw cane sugar, or to taste
½ red chili, finely sliced

First make the pancakes: mix the rice flour with the turmeric, then gradually whisk in the coconut milk and 9 Tbsp [140 ml] chilled water to a smooth batter. Set aside to rest 30 minutes. Make the dipping sauce by combining all the ingredients with 2 Tbsp water.

Now for the filling. Heat a nonstick skillet over high heat with the oil. As it begins to smoke, add the mushrooms and toss for 1 minute. Set aside. Allow the pan to heat up again, then sear the leek 1 minute. Set aside.

Wipe the pan clean and return to the heat with another drop of oil. When it's hot, pour a ladle of batter into the pan and swirl it around to cover the base. Reduce the heat to medium and spoon 2 tsp oil around the edges to make it crispy.

Sprinkle a few mushrooms, leeks, Raw turnips with cilantro, and bean sprouts over half the pancake and cook 3 to 5 minutes, until the underside is very crispy and golden brown (if you don't do this, it will fall apart), then carefully fold over to enclose the filling. Don't worry if it tears a bit. Keep warm in a low oven at 225°F [110°C] while you cook the rest. Wrap pieces of the filled pancake and some mint in lettuce, then dip them in the sauce. Delicious.

STORAGE The Raw turnips are best eaten fresh, but both the batter and fillings will keep a few days in a sealed container in the refrigerator. The cooked and filled pancakes are best eaten immediately.

Pickled turnips in cider vinegar with mustard seeds

These go well with just about everything. Classically, they're served with falafel and kebabs. Makes one 3 cup [750 ml] jar.

10½ oz [300 g] turnips, ½ small beet, 7 Tbsp [100 ml] cider vinegar, 1 tsp mustard seeds, 1 tsp rapadura or raw cane sugar, 2 garlic cloves, 1 bay leaf

Top and tail the turnips and beet and remove the skins only if they're tough. Cut them into large batons. Combine the rest of the ingredients in a saucepan with 1¼ cups [275 ml] water and 2 Tbsp salt. Bring to a boil, stirring occasionally, then remove from the heat. Meanwhile, sterilize a 3 cup [750 ml] jar (see page 52). While the jar is hot, fill it with the turnips and beet, then top it up with the hot pickling liquor. Screw the lid on tightly. Once cooled they are ready to eat, but will keep in the refrigerator 1 month.

MORE PICKLED TURNIPS . . . AND LEFTOVERS
Falafel salad. If you have leftover falafels and salad, tear the falafel up and mix into the salad.

Falafel burger. Make the falafel mixture into 4 burger patty shapes and fry in a pan with a little light olive oil until they are browned and crispy, then turn and brown the other side. Eat in buns with hummus, roasted bell peppers, and Pickled turnips in cider vinegar with mustard seeds. Serves 4.

Falafel with winter slaw and yogurt

The pickled turnips are a vital component here. They bring the dish together and give it some serious tang. Serves 4.

For the slaw and salad bits
3½ oz [100 g] Pickled turnips in cider vinegar with mustard seeds
1 satsuma, peeled and pulled into segments
2 celery sticks, roughly sliced
3½ oz [100 g] Brussels sprouts, finely sliced
½ red onion, sliced
Leaves from 3 sprigs mint
3 sprigs parsley, chopped
Live natural yogurt, chili sauce, and flatbread, to serve

For the falafel
7 oz [200 g] dried chickpeas, soaked overnight
½ small onion, peeled and roughly chopped
1 garlic clove, roughly chopped
2 tsp cilantro, stalks and leaves roughly chopped
1 tsp cumin seeds, toasted (see page 163)
1½ Tbsp spelt flour
1 tsp baking powder
Flavorless vegetable oil, to deep-fry

Start with the falafel. Drain the chickpeas, allow them to dry a little, then put them in a blender with all the other falafel ingredients except the oil, adding 1 tsp salt. Blend 2 minutes to a rough paste. Roll into 16 to 20 small (¾ to 1 in [2 to 3 cm]) balls, cover and chill.

Now prepare the salad. Combine the satsuma, celery, Brussels sprouts, onion, and herbs. Season with a little salt. Set aside.

Fill a small, high-sided saucepan with ¾ to 1 in [2 to 3 cm] oil. The pan should be less than one-third full, to allow for the oil to bubble up when frying. Put it over medium heat. If you have an oil thermometer, bring the temperature to 350°F [180°C]. If not, then put a small amount of the falafel mixture into the oil. When it floats to the top and is bubbling a lot, the oil should be hot enough to fry.

Fry the falafel in batches of 6 or 7, so the oil doesn't drop too much in temperature, turning them after a minute or two. When the falafel are nutty and brown, remove them from the oil with a slotted spoon and place on paper towels to drain. Keep them warm in a low oven at 225°F [110°C] while you fry the others. Serve with the salad, yogurt, chili sauce, flatbread, and pickled turnips.

STORAGE The pickled turnips will keep in their sealed jar in the refrigerator 1 month. If you have too much falafel mixture, it's best to keep it raw and cook them from fresh when needed (see left for variations). Both the falafel mixture and the cooked falafels will keep in sealed containers in the refrigerator 3 days. Return cooked falafels to room temperature before serving.

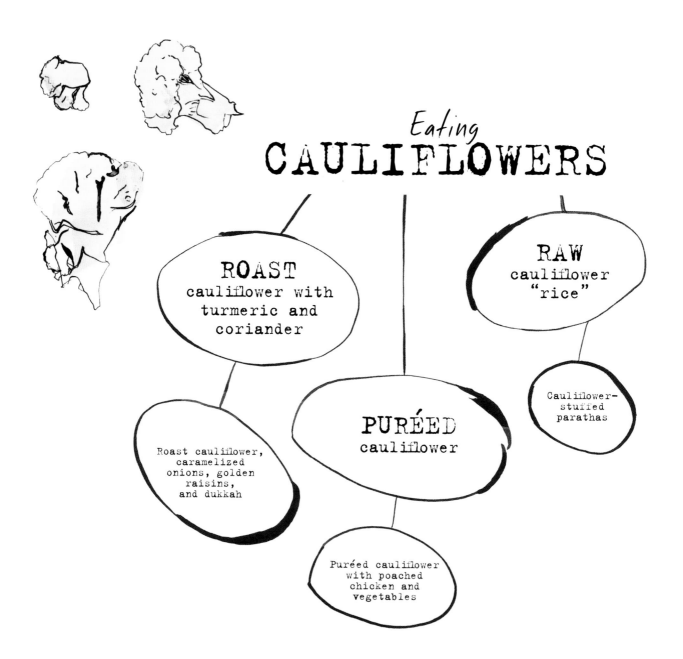

Eating
CAULIFLOWERS

ROAST
cauliflower with turmeric and coriander

RAW
cauliflower "rice"

Cauliflower-stuffed parathas

Roast cauliflower, caramelized onions, golden raisins, and dukkah

PURÉED
cauliflower

Puréed cauliflower with poached chicken and vegetables

December to March Cauliflower has had a kitchen reinvention in the past few years. Gone are the days of cheddar-laden cauli cheese and soggy, tasteless, overboiled florets. Hello smooth cauliflower purée (see page 167) with roasted scallops and truffle, roasted cauliflower with exotic spices and herbs (see right), and raw cauliflower "rice" sushi (see page 164).

Cauliflower is a crisp, subtly flavored vegetable that should be revered. Choose those with white (not yellowed) curds with plenty of the leaves that protect them from bruising, and store in the refrigerator in a plastic bag. Cauliflower stalks are just as tasty as the florets, so don't forget to add them to your dish; peel them first if the skin is a bit rough. The bigger green leaves can be tough and are best fed to the compost monster, but the smaller, yellower leaflets are delicious.

Roast cauliflower with turmeric and coriander

This spicy dish is a great winter warmer. It's deeply savory and has bold, rounded flavors. Trim the leaves from the cauliflower and keep to use as you would spring greens, or in Roast cauliflower, caramelized onions, golden raisins, and dukkah (see right). Serves 4 to 6 as a side dish.

1 cauliflower, light olive oil, ½ tsp turmeric, 1 tsp ground coriander

Preheat the oven to 350°F [180°C]. Cut the cauliflower into florets and the stalk into cubes (peel the stalk if the skin is tough). Place on a baking sheet and drizzle with the light olive oil. Sprinkle with the turmeric, coriander seeds, and some salt and pepper. Toss to coat with the spices and oil, then roast in the oven 20 to 30 minutes, or until the florets char slightly and soften inside.

MORE ROAST CAULIFLOWER . . . AND LEFTOVERS
Cauliflower baked with yogurt. You must try this. Preheat the oven to 350°F [180°C]. To 1 quantity Roast cauliflower with turmeric and coriander, add the wilted leaves of the cauliflower, 14 Tbsp [200 ml] natural live yogurt, 2 finely chopped garlic cloves, 1 tsp ground coriander, a squeeze of lemon juice, salt, and pepper. Mix and put into an earthenware dish. Sprinkle a little turmeric on top and put in the oven 25 minutes. Serves 4 to 6 as a side dish.

Aloo gobi. Make 1 quantity Roast cauliflower with turmeric and coriander and boil an equal quantity of potatoes until soft, then drain and cut them into 2 in [5 cm] cubes. Sauté 1 roughly chopped onion and 3 roughly chopped garlic cloves 10 minutes in light olive oil, adding 1 Tbsp garam masala. Add the potatoes and cauliflower and fry over medium heat until everything is hot right through. Add a handful of peas and 7 Tbsp [100 ml] water. Bring to a boil, stirring, then serve. Serves 4.

Roast cauliflower, caramelized onions, golden raisins, and dukkah

Dukkah is an Egyptian condiment that is served with olive oil and bread as a dip. Here it is used as a seasoning and really brings the dish to life. Serves 6.

For the salad
1 quantity Roast cauliflower with turmeric and coriander
1 large onion, sliced
Glug of light olive oil
1 tsp cumin seeds
¼ cup [50 g] golden or black raisins
Leaves from the cauliflower, left whole (use a few leaves of kale if you don't have the cauliflower leaves)

For the dukkah
2 Tbsp sesame seeds
1 Tbsp coriander seeds
1 tsp cumin seeds
4 tsp hazelnuts

To make the dukkah, toast every ingredient separately in a dry pan until it browns slightly, then pound them all together in a mortar and pestle until they are finely crushed. Be careful not to overblend, as you want the mixture to stay as a powder, not become an oily paste.

Sauté the onion in the light olive oil over medium heat 15 minutes with the cumin and a pinch of salt. Allow the onion to color, then add the golden raisins and cauliflower leaves, or kale, with the cauliflower. Turn all together to combine the flavors, cover, and allow the leaves to wilt 3 minutes. Serve hot or cold with a sprinkling of the dukkah.

STORAGE The dukkah will keep in a jar 1 month. Both the roast cauliflower and the salad will keep in a sealed container in the refrigerator 3 days. Reheat the roast cauliflower in an oven preheated to 350°F [180°C] until hot right through. Return the salad to room temperature before serving.

Raw cauliflower "rice"

A great way to eat raw cauliflower, this transforms the crunchy florets into a lovely salad. This technique also works well with carrots. Serves 2 to 4 as a side salad.

½ small cauliflower (about 7 oz [200 g]), 6 mint leaves, juice of ¼ lemon, 1 Tbsp extra virgin olive oil, pinch of cumin seeds

Pull the leaves from the cauliflower and finely chop the most tender of them along with the mint. (Compost the thicker leaves.) Break the cauliflower into small florets and cut the stalk into pieces (peel it only if the skin is tough). Blend the cauliflower, in batches, to a fine rice-like consistency. Dress with the lemon juice and extra virgin oil, then season with the cumin and some salt and stir in the chopped leaves. Serve as part of a lunch or meze, with flatbread and other vegetable salads.

MORE RAW CAULIFLOWER . . . AND LEFTOVERS
Celery root rice. Follow the cauliflower "rice" recipe using a peeled celery root, seasoning with caraway seeds instead of cumin. So good. Serves 4 as a side salad.

Other veg parathas. This paratha recipe is an incredibly useful weapon in your culinary armory. Any raw veggies are good inside, especially grated roots. And I have never known anyone turn down a hot paratha.

Cauliflower-stuffed parathas

These are sumptuous and simple to make. They serve parathas for breakfast in India with yogurt and pickled vegetables or mango chutney and I suggest you do the same. Excellent on a cold day. Makes 6 breads.

1 quantity Raw cauliflower "rice"
1 cup [125 g] wholemeal flour, plus more to dust
1 cup [125 g] spelt or all-purpose flour
2 tsp extra virgin olive oil
Butter

Mix together the flours, extra virgin oil, 1 tsp salt, and ½ cup [125 ml] water and knead into a dough. Cover and set aside 20 minutes to rest.

Split the dough into 6 balls. Place some wholemeal flour in a bowl, then dip a ball of dough into the flour and roll it around so it is covered in flour. Roll the dough to roughly an 3 in [8 cm] disc. Place 1 heaped Tbsp Raw cauliflower "rice" in the middle and bring the sides of the dough up around the cauliflower. Seal closed by pressing the dough together once again, creating a dough ball. Dip again in the flour, covering the ball, then roll out to about 6 in [15 cm]; don't worry if some of the filling breaks through. Dust with flour once more and set aside while you stuff and roll out the rest.

Heat a heavy-based skillet over medium heat. Add a touch of butter, then gently cook a paratha on one side a few minutes until browned. Flip and cook the other side, too. Keep warm while you cook the rest, then serve immediately.

STORAGE The cauliflower "rice" will keep in a sealed container in the refrigerator 3 days. Make and eat the parathas straightaway for best results, but they will also keep in the refrigerator 3 days. Reheat them, wrapped in foil, in an oven preheated to 350°F [180°C], 5 to 10 minutes.

COOK NATURAL Try raw food sushi. Make vegan nori rolls using Raw cauliflower "rice" as the filling. (Check out rolling techniques on YouTube.) Lay a sheet of nori on a work top and press on a ¼ in [5 mm] layer of cauliflower rice, leaving a border of nori at each end. Lay a thin line of your chosen filling from left to right along the middle: I like to use home-sprouted beans (see page 126) with a sprinkle of seeds and batons of raw artichoke heart, all dressed with a squeeze of lemon juice, but feel free to experiment with different raw veggies. Roll the sushi like a cigar, wetting the nori at one end to seal it. Cut into bite-size pieces and serve with soy sauce or tamari and a dab of wasabi.

Puréed cauliflower

This clean, unadulterated recipe captures the real essence of cauliflower, especially when you find a perfect snow-white specimen with perky, squeaky leaves. It works well with white fish and seafood, or as a comforting vegetable with any meal. Serves 4 to 6 as a side dish.

1 small cauliflower (about 1⅛ lb [500 g]), 1⅔ cups [400 ml] whole cow's, goat's, or almond milk, 1 bay leaf

Pull off the green leaves from the cauliflower. Cut the smaller leaves into rough pieces and compost the larger, tougher leaves. Break the cauliflower into florets. Peel the stalk only if it is tough, then cut it into pieces the same size as the florets. Put the cauliflower and smaller leaves into a small saucepan and add the milk and bay leaf. Cover and gently bring to a boil, then reduce the heat and simmer 10 minutes, or until tender when pierced with a knife. Remove the bay leaf. Blend, in batches, to a smooth purée (the blender should only be one-third full), using just enough of the milk to help the process and to get the consistency you want. Season carefully with salt.

MORE PURÉED CAULIFLOWER . . . AND LEFTOVERS
Chicken liver in red wine. I guarantee you this is a fantastic snack using the chicken liver. Very finely chop the chicken liver and 1 garlic clove. Gently fry with a sage leaf in a knob of butter 5 minutes, keeping the temperature low enough not to burn the garlic. Add a glug of red wine and allow it to reduce to a thick sauce. Repeat 3 or 4 times, cooking the liver 15 to 20 minutes in total. Serve on toast as a predinner snack. Serves 2 as a nibble.

Cauliflower soup. Make the Puréed cauliflower but use 2½ cups [600 ml] milk so it makes a soup when blended. Serve with a spoonful of live natural yogurt or cream and sprinkle a pinch of toasted cumin seeds (see page 163) on top. Serves 4.

Puréed cauliflower with poached chicken and vegetables

A great, warming alternative to a roast dinner. Cooked gently, the chicken is so tender. The broth can be kept in the refrigerator with any leftover meat to eat over the next few days. Serves 6 to 8.

1 quantity Puréed cauliflower
1 chicken, with giblets (2¼ to 3 lb [1 to 1.5 kg])
2 bay leaves
1 tsp fenugreek seeds or dried fenugreek leaves (optional)
8 small carrots
8 shallots
2 celery sticks, each cut into 4
8 garlic cloves

Preheat the oven to 300°F [150°C]. Choose a pot big enough to hold tightly the whole chicken as well as all the vegetables. Add the chicken and its giblets (apart from the liver), bay leaves, fenugreek, if using, and a generous pinch of salt, then cover with cold water. Gently bring to a boil, then cover and immediately reduce the heat to a low, trembling simmer. Leave 15 minutes.

Add the carrots, shallots, celery, and garlic. Cover once more and put into the oven 1 hour.

Remove from the oven and rest 20 to 25 minutes. Serve the chicken whole on a platter with the poached vegetables and garlic cloves and the hot cauliflower purée. Cooked like this, the heart and neck of the bird are treats, full of flavor.

STORAGE Both the cauliflower purée and the poached chicken and vegetables will keep 4 days in sealed containers in the refrigerator. Reheat the purée in a saucepan over a gentle heat. The chicken and vegetables are best reheated gently in their large pan with the broth, to help keep everything juicy.

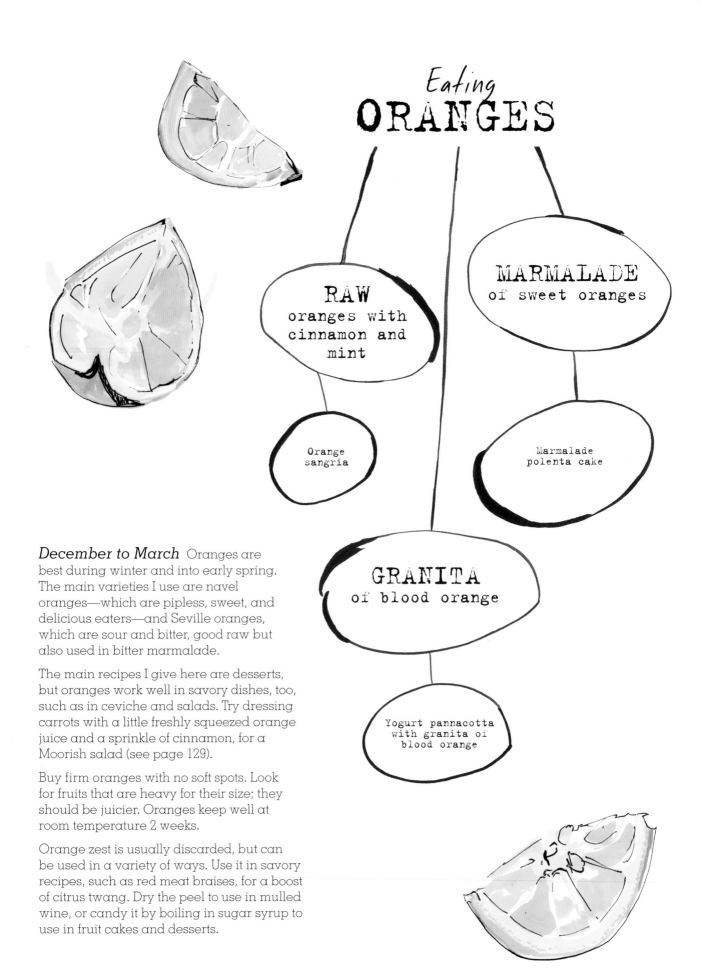

Eating ORANGES

RAW
oranges with cinnamon and mint

Orange sangria

MARMALADE
of sweet oranges

Marmalade polenta cake

GRANITA
of blood orange

Yogurt pannacotta with granita of blood orange

December to March Oranges are best during winter and into early spring. The main varieties I use are navel oranges—which are pipless, sweet, and delicious eaters—and Seville oranges, which are sour and bitter, good raw but also used in bitter marmalade.

The main recipes I give here are desserts, but oranges work well in savory dishes, too, such as in ceviche and salads. Try dressing carrots with a little freshly squeezed orange juice and a sprinkle of cinnamon, for a Moorish salad (see page 129).

Buy firm oranges with no soft spots. Look for fruits that are heavy for their size; they should be juicier. Oranges keep well at room temperature 2 weeks.

Orange zest is usually discarded, but can be used in a variety of ways. Use it in savory recipes, such as red meat braises, for a boost of citrus twang. Dry the peel to use in mulled wine, or candy it by boiling in sugar syrup to use in fruit cakes and desserts.

Granita of blood orange

Granita is a nice alternative to ice cream when cooking at home. It needs no special equipment and hits the sweet spot. Makes 4 small servings.

1⅔ lb [750 g] blood oranges (regular oranges will do), juice of ½ lemon, ⅓ cup [60 g] rapadura or raw cane sugar

Finely grate the zest of one orange, then squeeze 1 cup [250 ml] orange juice and squeeze the lemon half, too. Boil the sugar with 3½ Tbsp [50 ml] of the mixed juice, stirring until it has dissolved. Add to the rest of the juice with the orange zest and stir. Place in a shallow freezer-proof tub and cover. Put in the freezer for 3 or 4 hours until frozen. To serve, grate the block of frozen orange so that it becomes a slush.

MORE GRANITA . . . AND LEFTOVERS
Vanilla sugar. Keep the emptied vanilla pod, dry it in an airing cupboard or warm room, then put it in a pot of rapadura or raw cane sugar to infuse. This will keep indefinitely. Use the vanilla sugar in cakes and in any sweet recipe in place of extract.

Blood orange popsicle. Keep used yogurt pots, and cut slices of orange to fill the bases. Stand a wooden coffee stirrer or popsicle stick upright in the orange slice. Fill with the Granita mixture and put in the freezer 3 to 4 hours until frozen.

Yogurt pannacotta with granita of blood orange

This recipe is based on pannacotta, which actually means "cooked cream." However, for those of us that don't like to eat tubs of cream, this is a delicious and— I'd go as far as to say—healthy alternative. Serves 4.

1 quantity Granita of blood orange
2½ Tbsp agar agar flakes (from health food stores)
¼ cup [50 g] rapadura or raw cane sugar
1 vanilla pod or 1 tsp vanilla extract
7 Tbsp [100 ml] goat's or cow's milk
1¼ cups [300 ml] Greek yogurt

Pour 7 Tbsp [100 ml] water into a small saucepan and sprinkle the agar agar on top so that it floats. Turn the heat on and bring to a boil without stirring, then reduce to a simmer and stir 5 to 10 minutes, until the agar agar has dissolved. Add the sugar and stir until it, too, has dissolved. Cut the vanilla pod, if using, down its length and scrape the black seeds into the pan with the tip of a sharp knife, or add the vanilla extract, if using, then immediately remove it from the heat.

Add the milk and then the yogurt and stir thoroughly. The agar agar will begin setting, so work quickly now. Divide between 4 glasses. Put in the refrigerator to set at least 4 or 5 hours, then serve topped with a spoonful of the granita.

STORAGE The pannacotta will keep covered in the refrigerator 3 days. The granita will be good for 1 month in the freezer.

COOK NATURAL Agar agar is a great vegetarian replacement for gelatine, made from algae. It is used to set and thicken desserts such as pudding, ice cream, and jam. It is simple to use and is just as effective as gelatine. You can buy it from most health food stores. I like to use the powdered type the best, and I find that 1 Tbsp agar agar flakes to 7 Tbsp [100 ml] liquid gives a soft set, but check the package instructions.

Marmalade of sweet oranges

Immensely satisfying to make and relatively quick, considering the reward of owning 3 big jars of your own marmalade. Makes three 2 cup [500 ml] jars.

2¼ lb [1 kg] sweet oranges, 1 unwaxed lemon, 2¼ lb [1 kg] jam sugar

Squeeze the oranges and the lemon. Cut the citrus shells into quarters and then into ¹⁄₁₆ to ¼ in [3 to 5 mm] strips. Place the chopped peel, the juice and 2½ qt [2.5 L] water in a large pan, or a preserving pan. Bring to a boil, then reduce the heat and simmer 1 hour, to soften the peel. Meanwhile, sterilize three 2 cup [500 ml] jars (see page 52) and put a plate in the freezer. When the peel is soft, add the sugar to the pan. Boil 15 minutes, stirring regularly. To test for a set, take the plate out of the freezer and place 1 tsp of the marmalade on it. Put in the freezer 2 minutes. Remove from the freezer and push a line through the marmalade with your finger. If your finger cuts through cleanly, it is ready. If it is still runny, boil another 15 minutes and repeat the test, until it is set. Fill the hot jars with the hot marmalade and screw the lids on tightly. Let cool.

MORE MARMALADE . . . AND LEFTOVERS
Orange roast duck. A great classic dish. Preheat the oven to 350°F [180°C]. Smother a duck breast in a layer of fine cut marmalade and roast in the oven 20 minutes. Rest 5 minutes, then carve. Serves 1.

Marmalade ham. Get a green (unsmoked) or smoked ham, soak it if necessary, then simmer 20 minutes per 15¾ oz [450 g]. Drain. Smother a generous layer of marmalade over the skin and roast in an oven preheated to 340°F [170°C] about 20 minutes, until it caramelizes.

Marmalade polenta cake

This will give you a real sweet fix. I love the grainy texture of a polenta cake, which is made all the more delicious with the sticky marmalade. Serves 8 to 10.

8¾ oz [250 g] Marmalade of sweet oranges
⅞ cup [200 g] unsalted butter, at room temperature, plus more for the tin
1¼ cups [250 g] rapadura or raw cane sugar
1 large orange
7 oz [200 g] ground almonds
5¼ oz [150 g] fine polenta
½ tsp baking powder
3 eggs, lightly beaten

Preheat the oven to 340°F [170°C]. Butter a 9 to 10 in [22 to 25 cm] round cake tin, then sprinkle in half the sugar. Finely grate the zest from the orange, then carefully pare off and discard the white pith. Cut the orange horizontally into ⅜ in [1 cm] thick slices. Layer the slices of orange over the layer of sugar in the prepared tin.

Beat the butter with 3½ oz [100 g] of the marmalade, the other half of the sugar, the ground almonds, polenta, baking powder, orange zest, and eggs, then pour the batter into the tin.

Bake in the oven 40 to 50 minutes, until it doesn't wobble when you shake it. Remove from the oven and turn out while still warm, so the oranges are on top, carefully prizing off any orange slices that have stuck to the tin and arranging them back on top of the cake. Gently heat the remaining 5¼ oz [150 g] marmalade in a small saucepan. When melted, spread it over the orange slices. Eat warm or cold.

STORAGE Marmalade will keep more than 1 year in a sealed, sterilized jar. Once opened, it should keep at least 1 month. The cake will keep well 3 to 5 days in an airtight container.

Raw oranges with cinnamon and mint

This salad makes a great appetizer or light dessert and the muscovado sugar gives it a great caramel flavor. It is nice alongside fish or served with a tagine, too. Serves 2.

2 oranges, ¼ cup [50 g] rapadura or raw cane sugar, a few mint leaves, pinch of ground cinnamon, splash of Cointreau (optional)

Peel the skin and pith from the oranges with a sharp knife, then slice the oranges horizontally into discs about ⅜ in [1 cm] thick. Sprinkle with the sugar and tear over the mint leaves (this should be quite subtle, so go easy). Sprinkle with the cinnamon; again, a little will go far. Eat now, or add the Cointreau for a delicious simple dessert.

MORE RAW ORANGES . . . AND LEFTOVERS
Orange and fennel salad with olives. Make 1 quantity Raw oranges with cinnamon and mint, omitting the sugar and Cointreau. Thinly slice 1 bulb of fennel and toss it with the oranges. Top with some pitted black olives and a drizzle of extra virgin oil. Serves 4 as a side salad.

Ceviche. Make 1 quantity Raw oranges with cinnamon and mint, omitting the sugar and Cointreau. Finely chop 5¼ oz [150 g] filleted white fish (buy the freshest available and check online for up-to-date information on the best ethical choice). Mix with the orange salad and add a squeeze of lime juice. Leave 30 minutes for the fish to marinate and "cook" in the citrus juices, then serve, using Little Gem leaves as dishes if you like. Serves 4 as an appetizer.

Orange sangria

I discovered this recipe while drinking in a colonial bar in Granada, Nicaragua. It was the best sangria I'd ever had and the owner kindly gave me the recipe. Makes about 8 large glasses.

1 quantity Raw oranges with cinnamon and mint
1 bottle merlot
14 Tbsp [200 ml] freshly squeezed orange juice (5 to 6 oranges)
5 Tbsp [75 g] rapadura or raw cane sugar
5 tsp rum (optional)
5 tsp Cointreau
1 lime
1 lemon
1⅔ cups [400 ml] sparkling water
Mint sprigs, to serve

Pour the wine into a large pitcher or two and add the orange juice, sugar, rum (if using), and Cointreau. Stir to dissolve the sugar.

Cut the lime and lemon in halves. Squeeze half of each into the mixture, then cut the other halves into slices and add them, too. Put in the refrigerator to chill.

When you're ready to drink, add the sparkling water. Serve the sangria in glasses topped with a slice of Raw oranges with cinnamon and mint and a sprig of mint.

STORAGE The orange salad will keep a few days in a sealed container in the refrigerator (omit the mint leaves until serving, or they will oxidize and turn black), but is best eaten within a couple of hours.

Index

photograph by Joanna Casey

A massive thank you to Anne Furniss, Ed Griffiths, and everyone at Quadrille. This has been a steep learning curve for me and you've made it very enjoyable. Lucy Bannell is the best editor one could wish for and I've never felt in safer hands. Simon Davis helped develop and define the concept for the book and was an absolute joy to work with. Nicola Ellis did wonders turning our concept into a visually beautiful format.

The photo shoots were so fun, cooking with Marente Van Der Valk, working with Laura Edwards—who astounds me with her beautiful shots—and Tabitha Hawkins' amazing styling. I can't wait to work with you all again.

A big thank you to all the friends that helped me bring this book into existence. In particular Page Dykstra, Jason and Edwin Brooks, John Castley, Doug Fraser, and Niki Campbell for looking after everything I couldn't. Sanford Co-operative and my housemates have been incredibly understanding and helpful as I used the kitchen for cooking up test recipes and experimenting. Sarah Poffa, Stevo, Lee Simmons, Guillermo Just, Sine Skovsen, Tash Alpe, Jack Brindley, Robin Allison, and Libero Colimberti (who makes a mean fish pie).

I'd like to say a special thank you to Khanh Tran-Thanh for her honest advice, inspiration, and artichoke heart.

The crew at Poco festivals and our cafe in Bristol deserve a massive thank you. They have inspired many recipes in this book. Ben Pryor and Jen Best are the best partners and friends anyone could wish for and have been ultra-supportive. Without them, Poco and this book wouldn't exist. Adam Ashbourne is rocking the kitchen and should be credited for upstanding the quality of our food and ethics. Macky McCormack, thanks for doing an amazing job running the festivals without me while I've had my head down working on the book. Jonathan Pryor, thanks for being such a good friend, surf companion, and web designer. I'd also like to thank all our amazing suppliers in Bristol, including Scott, our butcher from Powells of Olverston.

I'd also like to thank my close family and friends who have helped me on the path with love and encouragement. Dodo, Anita Coplestone, Jane, Rich, Finn and Rowan Reddington, James and Emily Hunt, Ben Hodges, Cassy Olszewski, Whetham Allpress, Rose Murray, Sam Leeming, Mark Childs, Daniel Ferro, Joe Friday, Jo Vidler, Dan Bennet, Linzy the last Na Nakorn, Pip Ritchie, Spencer Rouse, Jamie Pike, Ed Dowding, Sophie Burns, Hannah Cowie, Champagne Charlie, Bill Aldridge, Pete Rands and Nell Knox, Nikandre Thea, Rosie Gardiner-Blunden, Dolly Theis, Ruth Dronfield, Louise Carver, Jim Whewell, Jen Holiday, Emily Elgar, Eloise Day, Freddy Drabble, Maria Rita Salvi and Oscar, Sam and Sam Clark, Marianna Leivaditaki, and all the River Cottage team.

Thank you to the Forgotten Feast team and volunteers: Tanya Moulson, Sebastian Lauret, Tito Bergamashi, Theresa Douthwright. Thank you also to our amazing suppliers and donators.

Thank you to all the amazing organizations that I have worked with in helping to reduce food waste: Tristram Stuart and Niki at Feeding the 5000, FareShare, FoodCycle, and LoveFoodHateWaste.

Most of all I'd like to thank our customers who have supported me, Poco, and the Forgotten Feast along the way.